Organisational Ambidexterity and Strategy

Across the last 50 years, there have been increasing studies on Organizational Ambidexterity (OA). However, there has been a disproportionate focus on the theory underpinning OA with less recourse to the implementation of OA. The primary purpose of this book is to close gaps in the understanding of Organizational Ambidexterity Implementation (OAI) and its relationship with organizational performance. It identifies key components crucial for successful OAI, including dynamic capabilities, organizational culture, organizational design and market orientation. The scope encompasses both qualitative and quantitative analysis, investigating the factors that drive or obstruct OAI and assessing performance disparities among organizations. This book is intended for academics, researchers, and professionals interested in corporate strategy with focus on the management of organizational resources and capabilities within organizational structure and design for performance improvement. It serves as a valuable resource for those seeking to understand how organizational culture, dynamic capabilities, market orientation, and design impact the successful implementation of ambidexterity and, consequently, overall organizational performance. Additionally, business leaders and managers can gain insights to help their organizations evaluate and enhance their abilities in these critical areas, ultimately fostering a culture of innovation and efficiency.

Imo Enang is a seasoned executive with more than 15 years of work experience in sectors such as FMCG, Banking, Academia, and Management Consulting. He has worked across Europe, the Middle East, and Africa, serving in diverse capacities comprising Commercial Operations, Strategic Marketing, as well as Strategic Operations and Organizational Design, which is at the core of his professional doctorate in Warwick Business School in the United Kingdom.

John M. Rudd is Professor of Marketing and Head of the Marketing Group at Warwick Business School. He serves on the Editorial Boards of the European Journal of Marketing and the Journal of Marketing Theory and Practice and has received numerous awards for teaching on undergraduate, postgraduate, and executive courses, and consults widely with large organizations and start-up organizations on marketing and strategic matters.

Routledge Studies in Management, Organizations and Society

This series presents innovative work grounded in new realities, addressing issues crucial to an understanding of the contemporary world. This is the world of organized societies, where boundaries between formal and informal, public and private, local and global organizations have been displaced or have vanished, along with other nineteenth century dichotomies and oppositions. Management, apart from becoming a specialized profession for a growing number of people, is an everyday activity for most members of modern societies.

Similarly, at the level of enquiry, culture and technology, and literature and economics, can no longer be conceived as isolated intellectual fields; conventional canons and established mainstreams are contested. *Management, Organizations and Society* addresses these contemporary dynamics of transformation in a manner that transcends disciplinary boundaries, with books that will appeal to researchers, students and practitioners alike.

Recent titles in this series include:

Management, Conflict Resolution and Strategy
Coping with Stress at Work
Magdalena Kraczla and Anna Wziątek-Staśko

Organizational Development, Innovation, and Economy 5.0
Challenges in the Digital Era
Edited by Elżbieta Jędrych and Agnieszka Rzepka

Ending Slavery in the Corporate Supply Chain
Storytelling, Leadership, and the Coalition of Immokalee Workers
Richard Herder

Organisational Ambidexterity and Strategy
Design, Structure and Implementation
Imo Enang and John M. Rudd

Organisational Ambidexterity and Strategy

Design, Structure and Implementation

Imo Enang and John M. Rudd

Routledge
Taylor & Francis Group
NEW YORK AND LONDON

First published 2025
by Routledge
605 Third Avenue, New York, NY 10158

and by Routledge
4 Park Square, Milton Park, Abingdon, Oxon, OX14 4RN

Routledge is an imprint of the Taylor & Francis Group, an informa business

Library of Congress Cataloging-in-Publication Data
Names: Enang, Imo, author. | Rudd, John M., author.
Title: Organisational ambidexterity and strategy : design, structure and implementation / Imo Enang and John M. Rudd.
Description: New York, NY : Routledge, 2025. | Series: Routledge studies in management, organizations and society | Includes bibliographical references and index.
Identifiers: LCCN 2024025820 | ISBN 9781032782201 (hardback) | ISBN 9781032785042 (paperback) | ISBN 9781003488224 (ebook)
Subjects: LCSH: Organization. | Management.
Classification: LCC HD31.2 .E53 2025 | DDC 658—dc23/eng/20240814
LC record available at https://lccn.loc.gov/2024025820

ISBN: 978-1-032-78220-1 (hbk)
ISBN: 978-1-032-78504-2 (pbk)
ISBN: 978-1-003-48822-4 (ebk)

DOI: 10.4324/9781003488224

Typeset in Galliard Pro
by Apex CoVantage, LLC

Contents

Figures

Tables

Abbreviations

CEO	Chief Executive Officer
DMC	Dynamic Managerial Capability
HRD	Human Resource Development
IT	Information Technology
MBV	Market-Based View
MNC	Multinational Corporation
OA	Organizational Ambidexterity
OAI	Organizational Ambidexterity Implementation
OAMM	OA Maturity Model
R&D	Research and Development
RBA	Resource-Based Approach
SIE	Strategy Implementation Effectiveness

Foreword

It is with great pride and personal reflection that I write this foreword for *Organisational Ambidexterity and Strategy: Design, Structure and Implementation*, a groundbreaking book authored by Dr Imo Enang. Having had the privilege of firsthand being part of Imo's growth and development during his tenure at Procter & Gamble, I have seen him evolve into a thought leader whose understanding of strategic business challenges and organizational dynamics is truly world-class. Imo has been, and continues to be, a mentee whose intellectual rigor and determination stand out in every endeavour he pursues.

This book encapsulates the essence of what it takes to be a successful strategist in today's complex, ever-evolving business environment. Having led multiple business transformations across a Fortune 500 company, I can attest to the necessity of balancing immediate operational needs with long-term strategic plan—what this book so eloquently defines as organizational ambidexterity. Imo expertly explores not just the theory, but more critically, the operationalizing of ambidexterity in driving organizational performance.

Imo's work is a must read for academics and corporate professionals alike. He dives deep into the multifaceted components of strategy, dynamic capabilities, market orientation, and organizational design—all within the framework of ambidexterity. His ability to blend quantitative analysis with rich qualitative insights sets this book apart as a must-read for anyone aspiring to understand or implement strategic ambidexterity within their organization.

Imo's work is both practical and visionary. This book is a reflection of his journey from commercial operations and strategic marketing to becoming a seasoned strategist. His clarity of thought and attention to the nuanced details of organizational performance are evident in every chapter of this book. He challenges readers not only to consider the dynamics of exploration and exploitation but also to reflect on how culture, leadership, and structure enable success in volatile and competitive markets.

What stands out most is the actionable wisdom embedded in this book. Imo provides readers with both a theoretical framework and concrete steps to foster a culture of innovation while maintaining efficiency. This is the hallmark of great strategy—leveraging today's strengths while positioning for tomorrow's opportunities to remain dynamic in the market. I have no doubt that this work will serve as a guiding light for many leaders seeking to successfully navigate the complexity of modern business landscapes.

This book is not just a scholarly achievement but a strategic tool for driving phenomenal business results. I commend Imo for his tireless work, and I trust that readers will find it as enlightening and impactful as I have.

Magesvaran Suranjan
Retired President, Asia Pacific, Middle East,
India, and Africa, Procter & Gamble

Preface

In this book, we delve into the heart of organizational ambidexterity (OA), revealing the intricacies of its implementation – the 'black box' that has long intrigued scholars and practitioners alike. While the theoretical underpinnings of OA have been extensively explored through hundreds of peer-reviewed articles, textbooks, and conference papers, a comprehensive guide to its practical application remains elusive. Our aim is to bridge this gap, bringing the same level of rigor, depth, and insight to the implementation of OA.

Designed with clarity in mind, this text leverages storytelling and a conversational tone to enhance engagement and understanding. It draws upon an extensive array of surveys and reviews, combined with the authors' wealth of managerial expertise and teaching experience, to offer a nuanced, comprehensive, and accessible exploration of OA strategies in the realm of design, structure, and implementation. "Organizational Ambidexterity and Strategy: Design, Structure & Implementation" promises a balanced discourse, enriched with both theoretical frameworks and actionable insights critical for strategists.

The Philosophy Behind This Book

The academic exploration of OA has undoubtedly shed light on its potential as a managerial tool. However, a significant chasm exists between theory and practice, leaving many to ponder the actionable steps towards harnessing OA effectively. This book endeavors to fill these voids, examining the pivotal factors that facilitate or hinder the successful implementation of OA and its impact on organizational performance.

Herein lies the essence of our text: to demystify OA by outlining evidence-based methodologies, underpinned by data gathered through multifaceted research stages. This journey begins with qualitative interviews from 50 senior managers across various industries, complemented by advanced quantitative analyses and machine learning techniques.

The thematic analysis distills four critical components for successful OA implementation: organizational design, market orientation, organizational capabilities, and culture. Further, we dissect the drivers and barriers to OA, delineating the contrasts between high- and low-performing entities. Through covariance analysis, we illuminate the relationships between key factors and OA, highlighting the pivotal role of dynamic capabilities and organizational culture. Performance variations, as evidenced by turnover rates, are examined through sample t-tests, reinforcing the interconnectedness of OA, organizational performance, and the foundational elements of culture, capabilities, and design.

Moreover, this study showcases the application of machine learning (WEKA) as a potent diagnostic tool for enhancing performance, underscoring the criticality of organizational culture, dynamic capabilities, market orientation, and design in optimizing OA and, by extension, performance.

Through this text, we aspire not only to contribute to the academic discourse but also to offer a practical guide that empowers leaders to navigate the complexities of OA with confidence and clarity.

Structure of the Book

Crafting a narrative that captures the complexities of OA in a manner that's both comprehensive and relatable is crucial in communicating these concepts effectively. The journey of an organization, particularly one navigating through the evolving paradigms of OA, is emblematic of the strategic agility required in contemporary business environments.

The crux of OA, as embodied by the Digital Dreamers, hinges on the nuanced understanding of its varying forms and their appropriate application. It's about discerning which approach – or combination thereof – aligns with the organization's strategic objectives, cultural dynamics, and market imperatives.

Sequential ambidexterity, with its phased oscillation between exploration and exploitation, may offer the stability and predictability necessary during a company's nascent or consolidation phases. On the other hand, structural ambidexterity, with its parallel processing capabilities, can fuel a more aggressive growth strategy. Contextual ambidexterity, however, infuses agility into the organizational fabric, engendering a responsive and adaptive culture capable of weathering both incremental and disruptive market shifts.

As an advisor in this field, I'd underscore the importance of strategic fit – not only within the organization's current lifecycle but also as a proactive posture toward future market dynamics. It's essential to cultivate a robust internal ecosystem where the elements of OA are not static but evolve as the organization grows.

Additionally, embracing OA necessitates a keen awareness of internal capabilities and market orientations, ensuring that these strategies are not pursued in isolation but are deeply integrated into the company's operational ethos and strategic vision.

The narrative of the Digital Dreamers is more than a case study; it serves as a microcosm of the strategic dexterity required in today's business landscape, where adaptability and alignment are the cornerstones of sustainable success. As we continue to examine and learn from such narratives, we contribute to the ever-expanding repository of knowledge that shapes our understanding of strategic management in complex environments.

Acknowledgments

I am grateful and fortunate to have had the following individuals whose unwavering support and guidance have been immeasurable on this journey:

- Prof. John M. Rudd, my Doctoral supervisor at Warwick Business School (WBS), whose unwavering support and expertise has been incredible.
- Prof. Nick Lee, Dr. Neil Shepherd, and Prof. Mark Johnson, whose insights have significantly refined my ideas.
- My colleagues across WBS Cohorts 1–7, whose collaborative efforts and shared knowledge have been enriching.
- The 50 interview and 408 survey respondents, whose contributions have greatly enhanced my understanding.
- The organizations and individuals providing access to case studies, whose support has advanced our comprehension.
- My family – parents John and Glory Enang, siblings Ime, Inem, Dr. Ini-obong, and Dr. Etieno Enang, wife Ufumwen, and children Edidem, Efe Zoe, and Andikan – for their unwavering support.
- Dr. Sree Beg, Prof. Mohammed Rafiq, Prof. Sunitha Narendran, and Prof. Lola Dada, for their invaluable mentorship and guidance throughout this journey.
- Dr. Rabi Fakunle and Teniola Phillips for their thorough reviews. I completely appreciate your support.

1 Introduction

DOI: 10.4324/9781003488224-1

"Organizational Ambidexterity conducts the harmony between an organization's rhythmic tradition and the melody of its innovation".

Foundational Inquiry

Organizational ambidexterity refers to the ability of organizations to balance the pursuit of both exploration and exploitation activities, with the goal of improving organizational performance. According to a study by O'Reilly and Tushman (2004a), organizations that effectively balance exploration and exploitation activities outperform organizations that do not. The authors found that "[o]rganizations that are ambidextrous in the sense of being able to engage in both exploration and exploitation are more likely to outperform organizations that specialize in either exploration or exploitation".

Dolph Schayes was one of the greatest Jewish basketball players of all time. During an interview with the media, he said, "I broke my right wrist but I was able to catch the ball and stabilize it so I was able to develop a left hand. My bread and butter was outside shooting and driving to the basket. Once my right wrist healed, I found myself being ambidextrous. I was able to drive to the right and if they overplayed me, I drove left, so I drove them crazy because they didn't know how to play me". According to him, this became a tremendous advantage.

> "The real secret to my success was I could shoot with either hand. Ironically, I became ambidextrous as a direct result of breaking my right hand"
> Dolph Schayes ~ Jewish Basketball Player (2011)

This anecdote summarizes the spirit and projection of this book, which seeks to extend existing knowledge, creating theoretical and practical contributions to OAI.

OA is a critical concern for organizations globally, as they strive to balance short-term efficiency with long-term innovation in the face of an ever-changing business environment. However, while the concept of ambidexterity is widely recognized, its implementation remains a challenge for organizations around the world. In rapidly changing [high velocity] business environments, organizations must consider multiple factors such as exploring new opportunities, new processes, and new markets while exploiting existing product offerings, processes, and mature markets to maximize efficiencies (Agostini et al., 2016; Eisenhardt et al., 2010; Turner et al., 2013). In trying to understand these phenomena, academics cite OA [OA] as an explanatory concept. However, little theory development is available around how organizations implement this important concept (Andriopoulos & Lewis, 2009; O'Reilly & Tushman, 2011).

A study by Covin and Slevin (1991) found that "ambidextrous organizations are more likely to achieve superior performance compared to organizations that are not ambidextrous". The authors also argue that organizations that successfully implement ambidexterity can achieve a competitive advantage by balancing their focus on exploration and exploitation.

However, the relationship between OA and performance remains a topic of ongoing research and investigation. A study by Hu and Wang (2018) found that the impact of ambidexterity on performance varies depending on the context and specific circumstances relevant to the organization. The authors stated that "the relationship between ambidexterity and performance is complex and contingent and is influenced by the nature of the business environment and the type of resources and capabilities involved".

The literature is replete with insights into the drivers, moderators and consequences of OA but has little to say about how senior managers should deploy resources or activity, that is, how these ideas are indeed implemented or could be implemented by managers in their organizations (Roglinger et al., 2018a).

Competing views on the construct of OA have also been posited in the literature, with specific references to exploration and exploitation. While Raisch and Birkinshaw (2008) suggested that exploration and exploitation happen simultaneously, Floyd and Lane (2000) saw exploitation and exploration as interdependent processes that need to be combined and embedded in organizations to generate synergistic outcomes. Benner and Tushman (2003) opined that both exploitation and exploration processes may be harmed by difficulties in realizing strategic integration across independent firms. Christensen and Bower (1996) stated that firms cannot simultaneously engage in both exploratory and exploitative endeavors. Gibson and Birkinshaw (2004), on the other hand, argued that OA can be observed from a contextual perspective and thus through the lens of alignment and adaptability. These divergent views are problematic in that while there is merit in the amount of theory building in this important area, there is no "common" concept of OA agreed in the literature. Additionally, empirical testing in this area has yielded equivocal results, highlighting the possibility of unexplored/additional themes. OA is a critical concern for organizations globally as they strive to balance short-term efficiency with long-term innovation in the face of an ever-changing business environment. However, while the concept of ambidexterity is widely recognized, its implementation remains a challenge for organizations around the world.

Previous studies on OA have primarily focused on local or regional perspectives, with limited attention given to the wider global context. This has led to a gap in our understanding of the unique challenges and opportunities that organizations face in implementing ambidexterity on a global scale.

Foundational Theories

OA refers to the ability of organizations to balance the simultaneous pursuit of exploration and exploitation activities. The concept of ambidexterity has gained significant attention in the literature as a way to improve organizational performance. According to O'Reilly and Tushman (2004b), "organizations that are ambidextrous in the sense of being able to engage in both exploration and exploitation are more likely to outperform organizations that specialize in either exploration or exploitation".

The theoretical foundations of ambidexterity are based on the resource-based view of the firm, which argues organizations can achieve competitive advantage by leveraging unique resources and capabilities. Covin and Slevin (1991) postulated that "ambidextrous organizations are more likely to achieve superior performance compared to organizations that are not ambidextrous". They suggested that organizations that successfully implement ambidexterity can achieve a competitive advantage by balancing their focus on exploration and exploitation.

However, the relationship between OA and performance remains a topic of ongoing research and investigation. Hu and Wang (2018) found that the relationship that exists between ambidexterity and performance is complex and contingent and is influenced by both the nature of the business environment and the type of resources and capabilities involved.

Ambidexterity theory proposes that organizations can achieve both exploration and exploitation by creating separate systems for each, while maintaining a coherent overall strategy. Exploration activities involve the development of new products, services, and markets, while exploitation activities focus on improving existing products, services, and processes.

Studies have shown that organizations that are ambidextrous have a supportive culture that values both exploration and exploitation, leaders who encourage both types of activities, flexible structures that enable exploration and exploitation, and effective communication systems that facilitate the exchange of information and ideas within the organization.

Some studies have found a positive relationship between ambidexterity and performance, while others have found a more complex relationship, with the effect of ambidexterity on performance varying depending on the business context and specific circumstances.

Gaps in Existing Theoretical Knowledge

Despite growing interest in OA, there is a shortfall in the extant theoretical knowledge regarding OAI and its impact on organizational performance. While previous submissions have identified the importance of leadership, structure, and communication in OAI; the interplay between these factors and their impact on organizational performance are less well explored empirically.

This text aims to address these gaps by exploring the application of open access and its effects on organizational performance. The purpose of this study is to provide fresh perspectives on the fundamental causes of OAI and its impact on organizational performance.

Exploration Synopsis

The significance of successful OAI cannot be overstated as it is crucial for organizational longevity. However, current research on OAI is limited and provides very little practical guidance for managers seeking to implement OA in their organizations. Instead, it focuses mainly on understanding drivers, moderators, and consequences. This lack of understanding leads to a lack of clarity surrounding the variability in sources of survival and the effectiveness of OAI.

Despite the importance of OAI for organizational success, existing research presents little guidance for managers looking to implement OAI in their organizations. Studies in this area concentrate on exploring drivers, moderators, and consequences but ignore the actual process of OAI, which is often treated as a "black box". Therefore, there is a need for further research to provide practical insights and guidance to managers on OAI. This text would attempt to fill the gap in the literature on how to effectively implement OA and translate it into improved performance (Smith, 2018).

Conclusion and Summary

OA, akin to Dolph Schayes' basketball prowess, is crucial for balancing exploration and exploitation, likened to shooting with both hands. While some studies support its benefits, caution is advised due to environmental and resource factors, echoing Hu and Wang's findings. Despite its significance, organizations globally struggle to implement it effectively, likened to athletes mastering a new skill. This text aims to bridge this gap by offering practical insights for managers navigating this complex terrain and serves as a springboard for the ensuing literature review, setting the stage for a detailed exploration of prior studies on OAI. As the saying goes, "Rome wasn't built in a day", emphasizing the need for patience and perseverance in achieving OA amidst challenges.

The exploration of OA in the introduction sets the stage for a deeper dive into the concept, its antecedents, consequences, and moderators in Chapter 2. As organizations grapple with the challenges of balancing short-term efficiency and long-term innovation, the need for a comprehensive understanding of OA becomes increasingly evident. The divergent perspectives on the construct of OA, as highlighted in the introduction, underscore the complexity of the phenomenon and the necessity for further examination.

Building on the foundational theories and the identified gaps in existing knowledge, Chapter 2 will delve into the various facets of OA, drawing insights from scholarly debates and real-world examples. The chapter will explore the types of OA, the drivers of ambidexterity, and the interplay between OA and related themes such as dynamic capabilities and organizational learning.

2 The Concept of Organizational Ambidexterity (OA)

"If you can't change the winds, adjust your sails".

– Unknown

Introduction

Building on the foundational concepts and theories introduced in the previous chapter, this chapter goes deeper into the multifaceted nature of organizational ambidexterity (OA). As highlighted in the introduction, OA is a critical concern for organizations striving to balance exploration and exploitation activities in an ever-changing business landscape. The divergent perspectives on the construct of OA, as well as the gaps in existing knowledge, necessitate a comprehensive examination of its antecedents, consequences, and moderators.

Through the story of the Digital Dreamers and their Chief Executive Officer Patricia, this chapter illustrates the practical application of OA and the challenges organizations face in navigating the tensions between exploration and exploitation. By examining the various types of OA, including sequential, structural, and contextual ambidexterity, the chapter provides a framework for understanding the different approaches organizations can adopt to achieve ambidexterity.

Furthermore, the chapter explores the relationship between OA and related themes, such as dynamic capabilities and organizational learning, shedding light on the complex interplay of factors that shape an organization's ability to balance short-term efficiency and long-term innovation. By building on the foundational concepts introduced in the previous chapter and providing a comprehensive overview of OA, this chapter sets the stage for a deeper exploration of the strategies and practices for effectively implementing OA in organizations.

The Digital Dreamers

Once upon a time, in a bustling city, there was a small but ambitious software startup called "The Digital Dreamers". The team was made up of

DOI: 10.4324/9781003488224-2

young, passionate individuals who had big dreams of creating innovative technologies that would make the world a better place. They had a few exciting projects in the works, but they were finding it challenging to stand out in the crowded market.

Patricia, the determined and curious CEO of the Digital Dreamers, knew that something had to change if they were to succeed. One day, while attending a business conference, she stumbled upon a workshop about "organizational ambidexterity". Intrigued, she listened attentively as the speaker explained the concept using a simple analogy:

> Imagine you had two powerful tools in your hands: a telescope and a magnifying glass. The telescope allows you to explore distant stars and discover new galaxies, while the magnifying glass helps you study the intricate details of the world around you. Organizational ambidexterity is like having both these tools at the same time – it's the ability to explore groundbreaking ideas (like using the telescope) while also making the most of what you already have (like using the magnifying glass).

A lightbulb went off in Patricia's mind. She realized that this was exactly what the Digital Dreamers needed to thrive in the ever-changing business landscape. Excited by this newfound knowledge, she returned to her team and shared her vision.

To test the waters, Patricia decided to run a small experiment. She assembled a team of three talented individuals from different departments and gave them a special project: to develop a cutting-edge mobile app that would complement their existing software offerings. The catch? They had to work on this project alongside their regular duties, ensuring that the day-to-day operations remained unaffected.

The results were promising. Not only did the team come up with a brilliant app idea, but they also managed to streamline some of their existing processes, saving the company both time and money. Encouraged by this success, Patricia knew it was time to scale up and fully embrace OA.

She restructured the Digital Dreamers into two distinct but interconnected teams: the "Explorers" and the "Optimizers". The Explorers were tasked with dreaming up revolutionary ideas and pursuing new market opportunities, while the Optimizers focused on refining and maximizing the efficiency of their existing products and services.

To ensure seamless collaboration and knowledge-sharing between the two teams, Patricia implemented a series of cross-functional meetings, workshops, and brainstorming sessions. She also created a shared digital platform where team members could exchange ideas, provide feedback, and track progress on various projects.

The impact of this new structure was felt almost immediately. Within six months, the Digital Dreamers had launched two groundbreaking products: a virtual reality training simulator for healthcare professionals and an AI-powered customer service chatbot. These innovations not only attracted a surge of new clients but also boosted the company's revenue by 35%.

Moreover, the Optimizers had streamlined the company's internal processes, reducing operational costs by 18% and increasing employee satisfaction scores by 22%. The Digital Dreamers were now not only exploring new frontiers but also maximizing the potential of their existing strengths.

In a rapidly evolving business environment, organizations encounter significant hurdles necessitating a delicate equilibrium between venturing into novel opportunities involving fresh solutions, processes, and markets, and capitalizing on existing product offerings, procedures, and mature markets to optimize efficiencies (Agostini et al., 2016; Jansen et al., 2009a; Eisenhardt et al., 2010; Moreno-Luzon et al., 2014; Turner et al., 2013). Over the course of several decades, scholarly attention has been extensively devoted to the concept of OA, with divergent perspectives emerging regarding its essence, antecedents, moderators, and ramifications (Linhart et al., 2020).

As the Digital Dreamers embraced OA under Patricia's guidance, the company began to soar to new heights. However, the journey was not without its challenges. Balancing the needs of the Explorers and Optimizers proved to be a delicate act, requiring constant vigilance and adaptation.

One of the first issues Patricia encountered was resource allocation. The Explorers, driven by their passion for innovation, often requested more funding and personnel for their projects. They argued that investing heavily in research and development was crucial for staying ahead of the curve in the fast-paced world of technology. On the other hand, the Optimizers emphasized the importance of channeling resources into refining existing products and streamlining processes to maximize efficiency and profitability.

Patricia found herself in a tug-of-war, trying to ensure that both teams had the resources they needed to thrive without compromising the overall financial stability of the company. She realized that striking the right balance required a deep understanding of the market, the company's long-term goals, and the potential risks and rewards of each investment.

To address this challenge, Patricia implemented a data-driven approach to resource allocation. She worked closely with the finance team to develop a dynamic budget that could adapt to the changing needs of the Explorers and Optimizers. She also instituted a quarterly review process, where both teams presented their progress, challenges, and resource requirements to a panel of experts who provided guidance and recommendations.

Another issue that arose was maintaining a cohesive company culture while fostering the distinct identities of the Explorers and Optimizers. The Explorers, with their focus on creativity and risk-taking, often favored a more relaxed and unconventional work environment. They thrived on brainstorming sessions, hackathons, and impromptu collaborations. The Optimizers, on the other hand, valued structure, discipline, and adherence to established processes. They found comfort in well-defined roles, regular check-ins, and measurable targets.

At times, these differences in work styles and priorities led to tension and miscommunication between the two teams. Patricia recognized that for OA to truly work, she needed to cultivate a shared sense of purpose and values that transcended the individual goals of the Explorers and Optimizers.

To bridge this gap, Patricia organized regular team-building activities and cross-functional workshops that encouraged employees from both teams to collaborate and learn from each other. She also implemented a mentorship program, pairing experienced Optimizers with up-and-coming Explorers, and vice versa. This fostered a sense of unity and mutual respect, as team members began to appreciate the unique skills and perspectives that each group brought to the table.

Despite these efforts, Patricia still grappled with the inherent paradox of OA: how to encourage exploration and experimentation while maintaining the stability and reliability that clients and stakeholders expected. She knew that the Digital Dreamers couldn't afford to alienate their existing customer base in pursuit of the next big thing, but she also recognized that playing it safe could lead to stagnation and obsolescence.

To strike this balance, Patricia implemented a "70–20–10" rule for project allocation. Under this model, 70% of the company's resources were dedicated to maintaining and optimizing existing products and services, 20% to incremental improvements and expansions, and 10% to high-risk, high-reward exploratory initiatives. This ensured that the Digital Dreamers could continue to deliver value to their current clients while also investing in future opportunities.

As Patricia navigated these challenges, she realized that the key to successful OA lay not in finding a perfect equilibrium, but in embracing the dynamic nature of the balancing act itself. Like a tightrope walker constantly adjusting their balance to maintain stability, she learned to be nimble and adaptable, always ready to shift strategies and resources in response to changing circumstances.

Through trial and error, open communication, and a willingness to learn from both successes and failures, Patricia and the Digital Dreamers continued to refine their approach to OA. They knew that the journey ahead would be filled with new challenges and opportunities, but they were confident that by leveraging the power of both the telescope and the magnifying glass, they could navigate the uncharted waters of innovation and achieve long-term success.

This strategic move by Patricia, our astute CEO, encapsulates the essence of OA – steering through the business tempest by balancing the sails of exploration and exploitation. Such a duality is echoed in scholarly debates and studies over the years, from the synergistic models of Raisch and Birkinshaw (2008) and Floyd and Lane (2000), to the more cautionary stances of Christensen and Bower (1996), emphasizing the complexity of navigating these waters.

Gupta et al. (2006) and Gibson and Birkinshaw (2004) further enrich the discourse, exploring the intricate alignments and adaptability required within an organization's structure to harness OA effectively. Despite varied viewpoints and suggestions – ranging from strategic alignment challenges in joint ventures (Benner & Tushman, 2003) to the prospects of spinning out explorative initiatives – the scholarly consensus on OA's core components remains as elusive as ever.

Initially, the literature presents conflicting views regarding the principal components of OA, namely exploration and exploitation. While Raisch and Birkinshaw (2008) argue for the simultaneous occurrence of exploration and exploitation, Floyd and Lane (2000) advocate for their interdependence, emphasizing the need for their integration to yield synergistic outcomes.

Benner and Tushman (2003) suggest that both exploration and exploitation processes may suffer from challenges in achieving strategic alignment across independent firms. Gupta et al. (2006) find the notion complex, attributing it to inconsistent alignments within organizations. Christensen and Bower (1996) adopt a pessimistic stance, proposing that firms must spin out exploratory ventures to enable success in both exploration and exploitation. Conversely, Gibson and Birkinshaw (2004) posit that OA can be understood contextually, focusing on alignment and adaptability as key lenses. As a result, a consistent viewpoint or consensus regarding the fundamental constituents of OA remains elusive across the scholarly landscape.

Just like the Digital Dreamers, we must learn to navigate the changing winds of life and make the most of our circumstances. Sometimes, this means changing course or even changing our sails, but it's all part of the journey.

Antecedents of OA

In the field of OA, there's a notable disparity in perspectives, not only regarding the construct itself but also concerning its antecedents. Raisch and Birkinshaw (2008) examine OA antecedents through three distinct lenses: Contextual Antecedents, which influence systems, processes, and beliefs, fostering alignment and adaptability across business units; Structural Antecedents, which introduce a trade-off between exploration and exploitation among business units; and Leadership-based Ambidexterity, driven by internal processes at the apex of management.

Contrary to this, Gibson and Birkinshaw (2004) argue for a broader conceptualization of antecedents, incorporating organizational context, structural elements, organizational culture, and organizational climate. This perspective posits that these elements collectively shape behavioral patterns within an organization.

Duncan (1976), an early advocate of 'Ambidexterity', proposed a strategy for achieving OA through sequential shifts in organizational structures, aimed at reconciling contradictory elements. March (1991) laid down foundational work, characterizing ambidexterity as the concurrent pursuit of exploration and exploitation, marking a pivotal point in the discourse.

In essence, the attainment of OA hinges on enabling organizations to oscillate between prolonged phases of stable change, emphasizing exploitation, intermittent bursts of radical change and accentuating exploration activities

Types of OA

Various typologies of OA have been proposed by scholars such as Tushman and O'Reilly III (2013b) and Wu (2018), encompassing sequential, structural/simultaneous, and contextual types. Additionally, Kortmann (2012) introduced innovative ambidexterity. This study will focus on structural, and contextual forms of ambidexterity.

OA involves simultaneously pursuing incremental and discontinuous innovation, achieving alignment and adaptability by establishing internally consistent architectures and cultures within business units. This approach enables organizations to navigate contradictory structures, processes, and cultures to effectively explore and exploit opportunities (Tushman & O'Reilly, 1996; Lubatkin et al., 2016; Gibson & Birkinshaw, 2004; Smith & Tushman, 2005a).

According to He and Wong (2004), ambidexterity requires balancing exploration and exploitation, operating efficiently in mature markets while developing new products and services for emerging markets. Similarly, Smith and Tushman (2005b) describe ambidextrous designs as integrating internally consistent architectures and cultures within business units to facilitate both exploration and exploitation.

Consequences of OA

The Digital Dreamers, leveraging uncertainty and adaptability as their guiding principles, found themselves at a crossroads when confronted with the various typologies of OA proposed by scholars like Tushman and O'Reilly III (2013b), Wu (2018), and Kortmann (2012).

As they advance deeper into the contextual, structural, and innovative forms of ambidexterity, the Digital Dreamers realized that their current approach aligned well with the principles of OA. They had been inadvertently pursuing both incremental and discontinuous innovation, navigating the balance between exploration and exploitation with agility.

However, the journey was not without its challenges. Some employees, accustomed to traditional modes of operation, struggled to adapt to this new mindset. They found it difficult to reconcile the need for stability and predictability with the call for innovation and flexibility. The clash between the old and the new threatened to disrupt the harmony within the organization.

Nevertheless, the Digital Dreamers persisted, recognizing that ambidexterity was not just a theoretical concept but a practical necessity in today's dynamic business landscape. They understood that achieving alignment and adaptability within their organizational structures and cultures was essential for sustained success.

Drawing from the insights of scholars like He and Wong (2004) and Smith and Tushman (2005a), the Digital Dreamers endeavored to strike a delicate balance between exploration and exploitation. They knew that effectively managing this duality would be key to their long-term performance and growth.

Moreover, they understood the importance of market orientation (MO) in driving their ambidextrous efforts forward. By focusing on understanding and meeting customer needs while also proactively seeking out new opportunities, they aimed to create superior value for their clients.

Yet, they were mindful of the criticisms leveled against market orientation, recognizing the potential pitfalls of being too focused on existing markets and customer demands. They embraced a comprehensive approach that encompassed both responsive and proactive elements, as advocated by Narver et al. (2004) and Peng et al. (2019).

Moderators of OA

According to the literature reviewed, we have several factors moderating/influencing OA and ultimately affecting the organization's performance. These are Market-Based View, specifically market orientation, and Resource-Based View comprising internal resources (Sebastian & Raisch, 2008). An overview of these concepts comprising both MBV and RBV and their connection with OA is provided below.

Market Orientation (MO)

Market orientation is defined as the firm's capability to generate, disseminate, and respond to intelligence pertaining to current and future customers (Kohli & Jaworski, 1990; Narver & Slater, 1990). We can infer that market orientation is a business approach in which the processes of product development and creation are focused on satisfying the needs of consumers. This consumer-centric approach is a departure from the conventional approach. This is an example of the MBV of Strategic Management.

Kohli and Jaworski (1990) and Narver and Slater (1990) proposed that senior managers' actions and attitudes influence employees who implement strategies. A market-oriented culture, as Hofstede (1997) describes it, emphasizes shared values focused on customer satisfaction, encouraging regular customer interactions, collaborative problem-solving, inquiries into customer needs, and open communication across functions. Our study follows Narver and Slater's view of market orientation, widely recognized in literature. They argued that market orientation includes competitor orientation, customer orientation, and inter-functional coordination, all crucial for effectively gathering and using market intelligence (Narver & Slater, 1990; Jaworski & Kohli, 1993).

Market orientation is a set of attitudes and skills that prioritizes serving the requirements of the customer and concentrates on gathering, using, and sharing knowledge about clients and competitors to enhance value (Narver & Slater, 1990). Alpkan et al. (2012) suggest that being market-oriented correlates with excellent performance. However, critics argue that market orientation may constrain organizations from expanding beyond current markets and inhibit innovation by excessively prioritizing existing client needs (Christensen & Bower, 1996).

As a result, Narver et al. (2004) proposed a two-part market orientation approach that is more complete. The first is responsive market orientation, which is defined as attempts to identify, comprehend, and serve the expressed demands of customers by a customer-led business.

The second type is proactive market orientation, where a company actively seeks to identify, understand, and address customers' unmet needs. Proactive market-oriented firms experiment with markets to uncover future needs or opportunities. Responsive market-oriented firms focus on current market data to understand and meet customers' expressed needs.

These two different market-oriented cultures call for different kinds of innovation. To meet the needs of the current customer base, minor modifications to the goods/services or improvements to factors like quality and turnaround time (also known as exploitative innovations) may be sufficient. On the other hand, to influence client preferences, wholly novel products/services or radical changes (also known as explorative innovations) are required. To resolve the contradictions between strategically pursuing exploitative and explorative innovation strategies, we adopt a comprehensive market approach that includes responsive and proactive elements (Peng et al., 2019).

Peng et al. (2019) argue that market orientation achieves a delicate equilibrium between exploration and exploitation, facilitating the creation

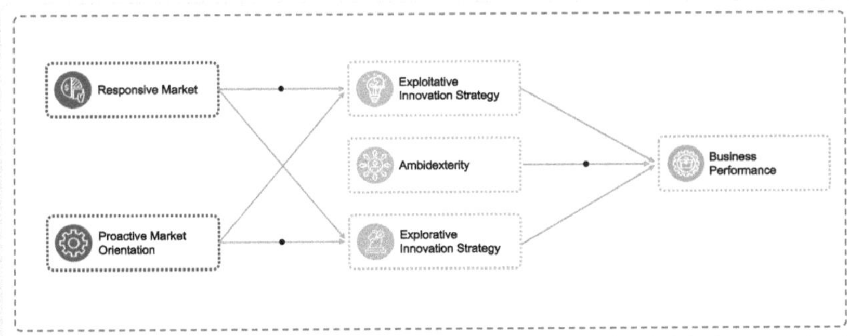

Figure 2.1 Model of Relations

Source: Alpkan et al. (2012)

and delivery of superior customer value. They suggest that firms benefit from two distinct and competing capabilities: exploration and exploitation. Engaging in both activities not only enhances operational efficiency (profitability, productivity, and market share) but also drives innovative organizational performance (environmental adaptation, new market development).

He et al. (2004) suggest that exploration, viewed through the lens of organizational learning theory, involves learning activities that go beyond current product-market knowledge to create new alternatives. These activities help firms acquire new knowledge, such as potential customer demand, technology, and market information, fostering innovation (Cao et al., 2009). However, persistently pursuing exploration alone isn't conducive to organizational development. Organizations engaged in exploration may divert resources from exploitation, incurring significant experimental costs and potentially failing to generate profits (March, 1991). Failure often drives organizations to embrace exploration strategies, as it catalyzes change and innovation (Levinthal & March, 1993).

Peng et al. (2019) suggest that the creation of new products typically requires a long-term approach. After introduction, new products undergo initial lifecycle stages, and their performance may not immediately cover operating costs. Thus, exploration allows firms to sustain market growth by overcoming product lifecycle constraints and inertia.

In consonance with the story of the Digital Dreamers, exploration and exploitation, the core components of OA, play a vital role in shaping organizational performance. Exploration was not just about venturing into the unknown but also about learning and innovation. They understood that failure was an inherent part of the exploration process, but they also recognized its potential to catalyze change and drive progress.

In the end, the Digital Dreamers remained committed to their journey towards ambidexterity, knowing that it was the key to unlocking new horizons of success in an ever-evolving digital landscape.

Resource Endowment

Resource endowment refers to the range and quality of resources at an organization's disposal to achieve its objectives (Chesbrough & Bogers, 2014). These resources encompass financial, physical, technological, human, and intangible assets such as reputation, brand, and culture. Resource endowment significantly influences an organization's ability to engage in open innovation initiatives, including open access (OA) (Johansson et al., 2017).

Studies indicate that resource endowment plays a crucial role in the adoption and success of OA within organizations. Firms with ample resources are better equipped financially and technically to pursue OA endeavors. They can invest in open-source software development, establish online collaboration platforms, or fund research and development projects that often lead to innovation.

Conversely, smaller firms may face limitations in resource availability compared to their larger counterparts, affecting their participation in OA initiatives (Pisano, 2019). These firms may struggle to allocate sufficient funds to research and development, build essential technical infrastructure, or engage in collaborative ventures to the same extent as larger firms.

Some studies suggest that smaller firms may have advantages in pursuing OA initiatives. They are often more agile, responsive to market changes and willing to take risks compared to larger organizations (Argote & Greve, 2007). The role of resource endowment in OA adoption and success is complex and context-dependent. Smaller firms benefit from the 'low height fall' paradigm, where the impact of failures is less severe due to their limited scope. Empirical studies support the relationship between resource endowment and OA initiatives. Johansson et al. (2017) found that firms with greater resources were more likely to engage in OA activities. West and Bogers (2017) noted that resource endowment significantly influences OA success, enabling firms to allocate necessary resources. Lichtenthaler and Ernst (2016) discovered a positive link between resource endowment and OA adoption in German manufacturing firms. Leiponen and Helfat (2010) observed that well-endowed firms in the software industry were more inclined to adopt open standards.

These studies provide empirical evidence of the relationship between resource endowment and the adoption and success of open access initiatives within organizations. Firms with greater resource endowment are more likely to engage in OA initiatives, as they have the resources to invest in the necessary infrastructure, technology, and human capital. Therefore, the availability of resources will play a role in the execution of OA within an organization. Large-scale firms may possess maximum resources which could afford them economies of scale whereas smaller firms may not possess this scale.

Organizational Scope

Organizational scope refers to the breadth of an organization's activities and operations, which can range from narrow, focusing on specific products or services, to broad, encompassing various products, services, and markets. Scholars like Rumelt (1974), Miller (1988b), and Collis and Montgomery (2008) have explored factors influencing organizational scope and its impact on performance. They argue that aligning scope with strategy and leveraging unique resources are critical for competitive advantage. Teece (2018) emphasizes the role of business models and dynamic capabilities in adapting to changing environments.

Lubatkin et al. (2006) suggest that large, diversified firms may benefit from structural ambidexterity, while smaller, focused firms may find leadership-based ambidexterity more suitable. Gibson and Birkinshaw (2004) note that smaller firms, with fewer hierarchical levels, often rely on top managers to address both exploitation and exploration opportunities. Conversely, large firms face more organizational complexity and external influences, potentially diluting the impact of top management integration.

The literature underscores the importance of aligning organizational scope with strategy, resources, and environment for superior performance. Flexibility and adaptability are crucial for responding to market changes and competitive dynamics.

Relationship Between OA and Related Themes

Several researchers have shown varying views on relationship streams associated with OA. Raisch and Birkinshaw (2008) talk about technological innovation and organizational adaptation, strategic management as well as organizational learning and design. Some establish links between OA and dynamic capabilities with O'Reilly and Tushman (2013), indicating that dynamic capability is the appropriate lens through which to view OA. Others have posited that OA is in fact a dynamic capability with O'Reilly and Tushman (2008) along with Teece (2006) highlighting that for firms to be successful at executing OA, they must possess and deploy the dynamic capabilities taxonomy of sensing, seizing, and reconfiguring. Based on the research by Eisenhardt and Martin (2000) as well as Teece et al. (1997), the ability to achieve ambidexterity has been said to lie at the heart of a firm's dynamic capabilities.

OA is therefore stated to require a coherent alignment of competencies, structures, processes, and cultures to engage in exploration, a contrasting congruent alignment focused on exploitation, and a senior leadership team with the cognitive and behavioral flexibility to establish and nurture both (O'Reilly & Tushman, 2008).

According to O'Reilly and Tushman (2008), ambidexterity only becomes a dynamic capability if the firm's exploitation and exploration activities are strategically integrated. Strategic integration requires a common set of values, a shared vision, and an overarching governance process. The literature has focused on three broad approaches that enable ambidexterity within an organization: structural solutions that allow two activities to be carried out in different organizational units, contextual solutions that allow two activities to be pursued within the same unit, and leadership-based solutions that make the top management team responsible for reconciling and responding to the tensions between the two activities.

Within the study of organizations, the term OA has been a very critical topic generating high-level interest by scholars over the last five decades. Tushman and O'Reilly (1996) proposed OA as the ability to simultaneously pursue both incremental and discontinuous innovation from hosting multiple contradictory structures, processes, and cultures in the same firm. Subsequently, the same duo O'Reilly and Tushman (2013) re-defined OA to be

> the ability of an organization to both explore and exploit – to compete in mature technologies and markets where efficiency, control, and incremental improvement are prized and to also compete in new technologies and markets where flexibility, autonomy, and experimentation are needed.

Early studies suggested ambidexterity was associated with firm performance (e.g., He & Wong, 2004; Katila & Ahuja, 2002; Lubatkin et al., 2006; Markides & Charitou, 2004). These studies have been followed by a large number of others both confirming the link between ambidexterity and firm performance and exploring the determinants of ambidexterity itself (e.g., Jansen et al., 2009a). Again, these studies have employed a range of methodologies from large-scale data collections (He & Wong, 2004; Venkatraman et al., 2006) to in-depth case studies (e.g., Garaus et al., 2012; Harreld et al., 2007; Raisch, 2008) to simulations (Fang et al., 2010).

Structural Ambidexterity

The literature defines structural ambidexterity as the establishment of differentiated units for exploitation and exploration with a carefully managed exploration–exploitation interface supporting cross-fertilization without cross-contamination (Hansen et al., 2019).

According to Alder and Heckscher (2015), in structural ambidexterity, sub-units are dedicated to business lines that focus on either exploration or exploitation types of goals. Each of these business-line sub-units is largely self-sufficient in its array of dedicated functional resources, and these sub-units collaborate directly only in targeted, tactical activities. Structural ambidexterity refers to the ability of an organization to simultaneously pursue two distinct types of innovation – exploitative and exploratory – while maintaining coherence and coordination across the organization. The literature on structural ambidexterity has examined various aspects of this concept, including the factors that enable or inhibit ambidexterity, the benefits and drawbacks of ambidexterity, and the different organizational structures and processes that can facilitate ambidexterity.

O'Reilly and Tushman (2008) propose a dynamic capability approach to structural ambidexterity, highlighting the need for organizations to balance exploitation and exploration over time and thus maintain competitive momentum.

In their paper, He and Wong (2004) test the ambidexterity hypothesis by examining the relationship between exploration and exploitation and firm performance. They find that while exploration has a positive effect on long-term performance, exploitation has a positive effect on short-term performance. Gibson and Birkinshaw (2004) examine the antecedents, consequences, and mediating role of OA, highlighting the importance of structural and cultural factors in facilitating ambidexterity. Raisch and Birkinshaw (2008) provide a comprehensive review of the literature on OA, highlighting the antecedents, outcomes, and moderators of ambidexterity. Tushman and O'Reilly (1996) introduce the concept of ambidextrous organizations and provide examples of different organizational structures and processes that can facilitate ambidexterity. The literature on Structural Ambidexterity highlights the importance of balancing exploration and exploitation to achieve long-term competitiveness and emphasizes the need for organizational structures and processes that support ambidexterity. It also underscores the role of leadership and culture in fostering a climate that enables ambidexterity.

O'Reilly and Tushman (2008) postulated that another method of establishing a balanced trade-off between both exploitation and exploration elements of OA is through the concurrent pursuit of both using separate subunits. This methodology typically characterized as *Structural Ambidexterity* entails not only separate structural units for exploration and exploitation but also different competencies, systems, incentives, processes, and cultures each internally aligned These structurally separated units are assembled by "common strategic intent, an overarching set of values, and targeted linking mechanisms to leverage shared assets" (O'Reilly & Tushman, 2013).

Drivers of Structural Ambidexterity

Pundits state that structural ambidexterity is grounded in the spatial separation of organizational units, which are each equipped with one of the paradoxical activities. As such, structural differentiation which is a key driver of structural ambidexterity in this regard is seen as "the state of segmentation of the organizational system into subsystems, each of which tends to develop particular attributes in relation to the requirements posed by its relevant external environment" and empirically confirm that this is one potential avenue to OA (Lawrence & Lorsch, 1967). Through structural differentiation, firms create "dual structures" that are separated by pragmatic boundaries. In this way, firms can benefit from different advantages. By ensuring the coexistence of inconsistent and paradoxical exploratory and exploitative efforts, configuring units to specific needs, and spatially separating these units with freedom and ownership over specific work activities to enable flexibility.

Results from earlier studies show a correlation between ambidexterity and firm performance and furthermore confirm that structural ambidexterity consists of autonomous structural units for exploration and exploitation, targeted integration to leverage assets, and an overarching vision to legitimize the need for exploration and exploitation (O'Reilly & Tushman, 2013; He & Wong, 2004; Markides & Charitou, 2004; Lubatkin et al., 2006). These can all be regarded as the hard skills necessary to ensure concurrent pursuit of both exploratory and exploitative elements of OA using separate sub-units. However, some authors have also postulated that leadership would be the soft element necessary to managing the tensions associated with multiple organizational alignments (O'Reilly & Tushman, 2011, 2013; Raisch et al., 2009; Lubatkin et al., 2006; O'Reilly et al., 2009; Smith & Tushman, 2005b).

According to Zaidi and Othman (2015), structurally ambidextrous firms separate the explorative elements of Ambidexterity from the exploitative elements, each with different management, processes, structures, and cultures. However, key to note here, as indicated by O'Reilly and Tushman (2014), is the fact that these are well integrated under the auspices of a senior management team to allow the structures to be "tightly coupled [within] subunits that are themselves loosely coupled with each other" (Benner & Tushman, 2003). For an organization to become structurally ambidextrous, one needs to have the senior teams (1) that have the ability to sense and understand different needs of businesses, (2) that are committed to implement ambidexterity, and (3) that communicate a clear vision to allow both explorative and exploitative NPD to coexist (O'Reilly & Tushman, 2004a).

The literature suggests that for simultaneous/structural ambidexterity to thrive, there needs to be a spatial separation, where dual and autonomous sub-unit structures for both exploitation and exploration are formed and coordinated by senior management. This mode suggests that dual and autonomous structures achieve optimal ambidexterity as the separated structures with autonomous teams, processes, systems, and cultures do not compete for resources with existing forces (Papachroni, 2015).

Sequential Ambidexterity

In contrast to structural ambidexterity, sequential ambidexterity would focus on the dynamic perspective on the "either exploitative or exploratory" decision established through the enabling mechanism of temporal separation. Therefore, sequential ambidexterity can be defined as the dynamic, temporal sequencing of exploitation and exploration time periods (Kortmann, 2012).

Brown and Eisenhardt (1997) indicate Sequential Ambidexterity as a "time-paced sequence of exploration and exploitation" being consistent with the dynamic capabilities view requiring organizations to establish dual temporal orientations comprising present and the future, whilst simultaneously balancing short- and long-term performance. According to Kortmann (2012), the effective pursuit of sequential ambidexterity would require firms to adapt organizational characteristics and architectures in accordance with exploitation and exploration. Therefore, sequential ambidexterity depends not only on a transformational capability that allows firms to switch between exploitative and exploratory tasks, but also on an implementation capability that caters for an appropriate organizational context to make the most of each period and explaining why OA is often characterized as a dynamic capability.

Drivers of Sequential Ambidexterity

Tushman and Romanelli (1985a) proposed that firms evolve through punctuated changes involving their adaptation to environmental shifts by re-aligning structures and processes in a sequential process. Sequential ambidexterity involves temporal switching as a way for firms to be ambidextrous. Further elaborating on this, Chou et al. (2014) posited that temporal switching capability is one of the dynamic capabilities that serve to assist an organization's switch from exploitation to exploration, and vice versa.

Numerous literatures on simultaneous Ambidexterity (O'Reilly & Tushman, 2013; Goossen et al., 2012; Chen & Katila, 2008) infer that sequential ambidexterity may occur over time and in more stable, slower moving business ecosystems. Leaning on practical examples, we see this trend in the tech world where engaging in re-aligning an organization's Research and Development activities to oscillate between exploration and exploitation becomes an uphill task (Chou et al., 2014).

In practice however, there isn't a pure plug and play process to this as organizations may rotate from one phase (exploitation) to another (exploration) and the ease within which they can execute this would be based on their inherent capability to maneuver. These temporal switching capabilities may be regarded in two forms – the first christened by Brown and Eisenhardt (1997) 'rhythmic, time-paced transition switching processes' which we may call oscillation and the second christened by Boumgarden et al. (2012) as 'vacillation' which we may call switching processes without specific time frequencies or rhythmic patterns.

Studies of sequential ambidexterity often focus on large-scale examples with the changes taking place over long time periods – Hewlett Packard over a 25-year period and USA Today online over a 15-year period being key examples offered by Boumgarden et al. (2012). We also see Laplume and Dass (2012) describe the evolution of a company over a 65-year period, in which for the first 25 years the firm emphasized sequential ambidexterity before entertaining the hybrid of both sequential and simultaneous modes of exploration and exploitation. Certain pundits have opined that sequential ambidexterity may be more useful in stable, slower moving environments (e.g., service industries) and for smaller firms that lack the resources to pursue simultaneous or sequential ambidexterity (Chen & Katila, 2008).

According to O'Reilly and Tushman (2008), previous studies have indicated that a mechanistic organization form benefits exploitation, while an organic one benefits exploration (O'Reilly & Tushman, 2008). As organizations hold varying organizational structures, it also follows these would induce the need for different structural requirements of exploitation and exploration. Behind these, scholars note that the key to successful sequential ambidexterity is to 'vacillate' between these dissimilar structures (Chou et al., 2014). By engaging in vacillation, an organization can pursue sequential ambidexterity to avoid organizational inertia (Boumgarden et al., 2012). To further complement and enable a smoother transition of this intermittent vacillation process, informal structures such as organizational culture, routines, and communication types can be added to the formal structures to bridge the gaps in facilitating the switching between exploration and exploitation (Boumgarden et al., 2012; Brown & Eisenhardt, 1997).

Contextual Ambidexterity

Gibson and Birkinshaw defined contextual ambidexterity as "the behavioral capacity to simultaneously demonstrate alignment and adaptability across an entire business unit". The ability to balance exploration and exploitation rests on an "organizational context characterized by an interaction of stretch, discipline, and trust" requiring a "supportive organizational context" that "encourages individuals to make their own judgments as to how to best divide their time between the conflicting demands for alignment and adaptability".

Contextual ambidexterity is a strategic management concept that emphasizes a firm's ability to balance exploration and exploitation activities within specific contexts or domains. Table 2.1 provides insights into the key principles and applications of contextual ambidexterity.

Lubatkin and colleagues examined the relationship between ambidexterity and performance in small- to medium-sized firms, with a particular focus on the role of top management team behavioral integration. They argue that effective top management team integration is essential for firms to achieve contextual ambidexterity and perform well over time.

Contextual ambidexterity is a strategic management concept that emphasizes a firm's ability to balance exploration and exploitation activities within

Table 2.1 Key Principles and Applications of Contextual Ambidexterity.

Author	*Title*	*Contribution*
1. O'Reilly and Tushman (2013)	OA: past, present, and future. Academy of Management Perspectives, 27(4), 324–338.	In this article, O'Reilly and Tushman review the concept of OA, including its origins, evolution, and current state of research. They argue that Contextual Ambidexterity is essential for firms to successfully navigate turbulent environments and create sustainable competitive advantage.
2. Raisch et al. (2009)	Taming the waters: the role of internal communication and coordination in the development of OA. Journal of Business Venturing, 24(5), 458–470.	Raisch and colleagues examined the role of internal communication and coordination in enabling firms to achieve Contextual Ambidexterity. They argued that effective communication and coordination mechanisms can help firms balance exploration and exploitation activities within specific contexts.
3. Gibson and Birkinshaw (2004)	The antecedents, consequences, and mediating role of OA. Academy of Management Journal, 47(2), 209–226.	Gibson and Birkinshaw examined the antecedents, consequences, and mediating factors of OA, including Contextual Ambidexterity. They argued that firms that achieve Contextual Ambidexterity are better able to adapt to changing market conditions and sustain competitive advantage over time
4. Gupta and Govindarajan (2000)	Knowledge flows within Multinational Corporations. Strategic Management Journal, 21(4), 473–496.	Gupta and Govindarajan examined the role of knowledge flows within MNCs in enabling firms to achieve Contextual Ambidexterity. They argued that effective knowledge transfer mechanisms can help firms balance exploration and exploitation activities across different contexts and domains
5. Lubatkin et al. (2006)	Ambidexterity and performance in small- to medium-sized firms: the pivotal role of top management team behavioral integration. Journal of Management, 32(5), 646–672.	Lubatkin and colleagues examined the relationship between ambidexterity and performance in small- to medium-sized firms, with a particular focus on the role of top management team behavioral integration. They argued that effective top management team integration is essential for firms to achieve Contextual Ambidexterity and perform well over time

Source: Modified from O'Reilly and Tushman (2003), Raisch and Birkinshaw (2009), Gibson and Birkinshaw (2004), Gupta and Govindarajan (2000) and Lubatkin et al. (2006)

specific contexts or domains (Lubatkin et al., 2006). Several authors have harmonized the characteristics of contextual ambidexterity as shown below:

1. Contextual ambidexterity is ambidexterity and not a one-size-fits-all solution. Different contexts may require different levels and types of ambidexterity, and firms need to tailor their strategies accordingly (He & Wong, 2020).

2. Contextual ambidexterity can lead to higher levels of innovation and performance, particularly when firms align their exploration and exploitation activities with their strategic priorities (Karami et al., 2020).
3. Firms that achieve contextual ambidexterity are more likely to succeed in entering new markets and diversifying their product/service portfolios (Chen & Chiu, 2020).
4. Effective leadership is critical for enabling firms to achieve contextual ambidexterity. Leaders need to foster a culture of experimentation and risk-taking while also ensuring that resources are allocated to support exploration and exploitation activities (Chen & Chiu, 2020).
5. Firms need to establish effective communication and coordination mechanisms to support contextual ambidexterity. This includes sharing knowledge and best practices across different business units and domains, as well as aligning incentives and performance metrics to support exploration and exploitation (He & Wong, 2020).
6. Contextual ambidexterity can be challenging to achieve and sustain, particularly in complex and dynamic environments. Firms need to continuously monitor and adapt their strategies to changing market conditions and technological developments (Karami et al., 2020).

Contextual ambidexterity highlights the importance of balancing exploration and exploitation activities within specific contexts to achieve sustained competitive advantage. Firms that can successfully achieve contextual ambidexterity can innovate, diversify, and adapt to changing market conditions, while also maintaining operational efficiency and stability.

Drivers of Contextual Ambidexterity

The TPS (Toyota Production System) would be a good way to visualize the term contextual ambidexterity. This was elaborated by Adler et al. (1999), who explained how workers simultaneously combine both routine tasks of automobile assembly (exploitation) alongside job rotations leading to increased efficiency (exploration) via what Adler et al. (1999) called the "meta-routines". Here, the broader management teams as well as inherent culture are established to provide to workers to drive the persuasion of both exploration and exploitation concurrently.

The academic discourse also points out that contextual ambidexterity can be achieved through the use of behavior and social means, where feature designing is created to enable and permit individuals to split their time between exploratory and exploitative activities (e.g., Gibson & Birkinshaw, 2004; Raisch & Birkinshaw, 2008; Raisch et al., 2009). It should be emphasized once again though that of the two models of ambidexterity, contextual ambidexterity is identified as more complex, and thus requires a bottom-up approach which emphasizes the active involvement and participation of individual team members as part of the organizational culture and context (Wang & Rafiq, 2014, p. 61). Amit and Schoemaker (1993) actually offered the view that even while viewed as a unique organizational capability, contextual ambidexterity is complex, time consuming to develop and is extensively dispersed (also cited in Wang & Rafiq, 2010, p. 61). This point is particularly relevant for this text as it accepts that due to multiple dimensions of entrenched values, structures, processes, and technical know-how, many organizations struggle with contexts that negatively affect the pursuit of ambidexterity (Birkinshaw & Gibson, 2004).

Given that this text positions ambidexterity with agility as dynamic capabilities to facilitate business transformation, the contextual dimensions of an organization task environment are of importance. In fact, the identification of contextual ambidexterity as a complex concept has dimensional value for the comprehension of the compounded complexity when ambidexterity is positioned with agility, another complex business capability. To clarify further, Table 2.2 shows various differences and/or similarities across sequential, simultaneous (structural), and contextual ambidexterity.

In our evolving story of the Digital Dreamers, the startup that had once mastered the winds of innovation and stability, we find a deeper layer to their journey: understanding and choosing the right type of OA for their mission.

Sequential ambidexterity was the first chapter of their journey. The Dreamers likened it to setting a course through the changing seasons – pursuing aggressive innovation during times of growth and focusing on fine-tuning their operations when consolidating their gains. This method was akin to a well-orchestrated symphony, with each section playing at the right moment under the conductor's baton – senior management. They cultivated a culture where precision in operational execution was as valued as the bold strokes of innovation. Each role was well-defined, and expertise was revered. However, this approach was akin to navigating with a map that changed only at each port of call, limiting the agility to respond to the unexpected squalls of the market.

As their horizons expanded, the Digital Dreamers embraced *structural ambidexterity*. They evolved their strategy, comparable to a ship designed with dual engines – one powering the steady course of their established business and the other propelling them into new exploratory ventures. This required the crew to be adept in different terrains, with the competence to leverage the strengths of stable operations whilst exploring uncharted territories. The executives, akin to a council of navigators, oversaw both engines' functioning, ensuring that neither drowned out the other's rhythm.

The most transformative phase for the Dreamers was adopting *contextual ambidexterity*. This approach was organic and democratic, much like a fleet of nimble vessels, each empowered to explore, discover, and react in real-time to the ocean's whims. Here, the philosophy of ambidexterity permeated every level of the organization. Junior managers and front-line staff became as integral to the decision-making process as senior management, steering their course with an eye on the horizon and a hand on the immediate tiller. Roles became more fluid, and individuals toggled between the stability of their core roles and the thrill of innovation. This fostered an ecosystem where adaptability was embedded into the organization's DNA, making agility not just a strategy but a way of corporate life.

Through it all, the Digital Dreamers learned that no single approach to OA could stand as a panacea. The market's vicissitudes demanded a dynamic blend of structures and contexts. They discovered that the robustness of their operations and the fertility of their innovations were interdependent, each feeding into and enriching the other. The balance of exploitation and exploration became a journey in itself – a meta-exploration of organizational identity and capability. As they charted their course through these varied paradigms of OA, they not only found success but also charted a path for others to follow in the complex, ever-shifting world of business strategy.

In their narrative, the Digital Dreamers demonstrate that the essence of OA lies not just in the structures built or the contexts fostered but in the very spirit of navigation that allows organizations to be nimble, decisive, and visionary – all at the same time.

The journey of an organization, particularly one navigating through the evolving paradigms of OA, is emblematic of the strategic agility required in contemporary business environments.

The crux of OA, as embodied by the Digital Dreamers, hinges on the nuanced understanding of its varying forms and their appropriate

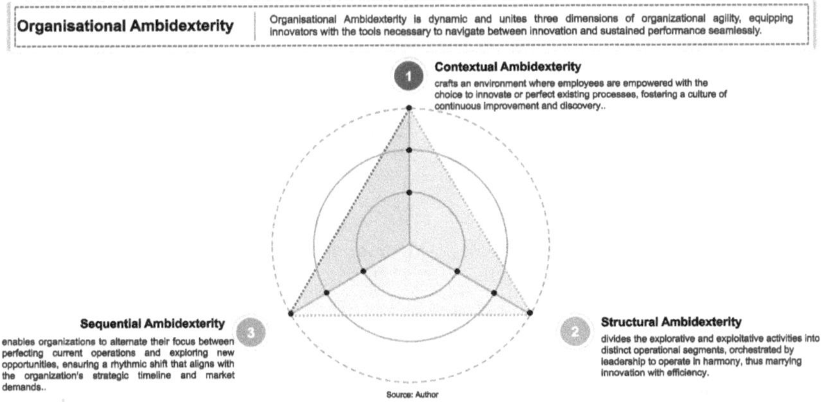

Figure 2.2 Organizational Ambidexterity.

application. It's about discerning which approach – or combination thereof – aligns with the organization's strategic objectives, cultural dynamics, and market imperatives.

Sequential ambidexterity, with its phased oscillation between exploration and exploitation, may offer the stability and predictability necessary during a company's nascent or consolidation phases. On the other hand, structural ambidexterity, with its parallel processing capabilities, can fuel a more aggressive growth strategy. Contextual ambidexterity, however, infuses agility into the organizational fabric, engendering a responsive and adaptive culture capable of weathering both incremental and disruptive market shifts.

As an advisor in this field, I'd underscore the importance of strategic fit – not only within the organization's current lifecycle but also as a proactive posture toward future market dynamics. It's essential to cultivate a robust internal ecosystem where the elements of OA are not static but evolve as the organization grows.

Additionally, embracing OA necessitates a keen awareness of internal capabilities and market orientations, ensuring that these strategies are not pursued in isolation but are deeply integrated into the company's operational ethos and strategic vision.

The narrative of the Digital Dreamers is more than a case study; it serves as a microcosm of the strategic dexterity required in today's business landscape, where adaptability and alignment are the cornerstones of sustainable success. As we continue to examine and learn from such narratives, we contribute to the ever-expanding repository of knowledge that shapes our understanding of strategic management in complex environments.

Table 2.2 Differences and Similarities across Sequential, Simultaneous (Structural) and Contextual Ambidexterity

Characteristics	*Sequential Ambidexterity*	*Structural Ambidexterity*	*Contextual Ambidexterity*
How is Ambidexterity Executed?	Temporal Shifting via Oscillation or Vacillation between Exploitation and Exploration	The Concurrent Pursuit of both Exploitation and Exploration using distinct Sub-Units	Executed via Social means with Individuals splitting time allotments between exploitation & exploration
What is time frame for execution?	Long term in nature and occurring in stable operations	Medium- to long-term endeavors	Based on Individual's predisposition – more likely short term
Decision Making	Executive/Senior Management	Executive/Senior Management	Junior Management/ Frontline Staff

(*Continued*)

Table 2.2 (Continued)

Characteristics	*Sequential Ambidexterity*	*Structural Ambidexterity*	*Contextual Ambidexterity*
The Role of Top Management	Define Charter and Operational Trade-offs between Exploitation & Exploration	Define Charter and Operational Trade-offs between Exploitation & Exploration	Foster the right organizational Ecosystem to enable Individuals Execute
Nature of Roles	Clearly Defined	Clearly Defined	Somewhat flexible
Skill Set Required for Execution	Specialists in Operational Execution	Specialists in Operational Execution	Generalist in Operational Execution

Source: Author

Conclusion

The in-depth exploration of OA in Chapter 2 highlights its significance as a strategic imperative for organizations navigating the complexities of dynamic environments. The Digital Dreamers' narrative illustrates the nuanced application of various OA approaches, underlining the necessity for organizations to align their OA strategies with their unique objectives, culture, and market conditions.

The chapter emphasizes the interdependence of exploration and exploitation activities, the pivotal role of leadership in nurturing an ambidextrous culture, and the importance of cultivating dynamic capabilities and a comprehensive market orientation.

As the chapter concludes, it becomes evident that OA is not a one-size-fits-all solution but rather an evolving journey that demands continuous adaptation and recalibration in response to internal and external factors. The insights garnered from this chapter lay the foundation for a deeper examination of OA as a strategy, its practical frameworks, and the interplay of various strategic management perspectives in the subsequent chapter.

By understanding the forms, drivers, and implications of OA, leaders can embark on a path towards sustained performance and competitive advantage in an ever-changing business landscape.

3 Organizational Ambidexterity as a Strategy

Introduction

Building upon the comprehensive understanding of Organizational Ambidexterity (OA) established in the previous chapter, Chapter 3 delves into the realm of OA as a strategy, exploring the practical frameworks and theoretical foundations that underpin its successful implementation. The chapter introduces the OA Maturity Model (OAMM) and Strategy Implementation Effectiveness (SIE) as key frameworks for assessing and enhancing OA in organizations, providing leaders with actionable insights for navigating the complexities of ambidexterity.

Furthermore, the chapter examines the interplay between the Market-Based View (MBV), Resource-Based View (RBV), operational capabilities, and dynamic capabilities, shedding light on how these perspectives shape an organization's ability to thrive in turbulent markets. By highlighting the importance of understanding organizational traps that can hinder OA implementation and presenting a synthesized view of the background logic of dynamic capabilities, the chapter equips leaders with the knowledge and tools necessary to overcome barriers and harness the power of ambidexterity.

The engaging narrative of Katrina's Kitchen serves as a testament to the practical application of these concepts, illustrating how the convergence of MBV, RBV, and dynamic capabilities can enable organizations to flourish amidst change. By building upon the insights from the previous chapter and providing a strategic lens for examining OA, Chapter 3 sets the stage for a profound exploration of the drivers and enablers of OA as a strategy, empowering organizations to embrace ambidexterity as a pathway to sustainable growth and success.

OAMM (OA Maturity Model)

OA is a vital capability for surviving in dynamic business environments by simultaneously pursuing exploitation, that is, continuous streamlining of

DOI: 10.4324/9781003488224-3

business processes, and exploration, that is, radical innovation of products, services, and processes (Roglinger et al., 2018a). During the last few years, OA knowledge has continuously matured, culminating insights into performance outcomes, antecedents, and moderators. Roglinger et al. (2018a) designed the OAMM using a design science research approach.

OAMM embraced a prescriptive purpose of use with the view of helping organizations select actionable practices by building on the six (6) core elements of Business Process Management (BPM) (i.e., strategic alignment, governance, methods, information technology, people, and culture). However, to structure the identified practices, OAMM was only able to lay the foundations for the structured development of OA capabilities and for future research in this area. Therefore, the enduring challenge of equipping managers with the right tools to enable them to implement OA effectively remains even more apparent than ever, as there remains a lack of guidance on how to put OA into practice and as such how to effectively implement OA.

SIE (Strategy Implementation Effectiveness)

The researcher sought therefore to unpick existing concepts analogously related to OA within the Strategy framework. One of such frameworks where extant literature has so far unpacked extensively would be the SIE.

Tawse and Tabesh (2021) systematically reviewed and synthesize findings in the extant strategy implementation literature to diligently derive an integrative framework comprised of three components:

(1) Actions through which managers influence the implementation process,
(2) Conditions necessary for SIE, and
(3) The underlying dynamic managerial capabilities to create the best possible combination of conditions by enacting the most appropriate managerial actions.

By explaining the relationships among these three components, they provided an introductory foundational framework on which to build future knowledge about this important field of inquiry.

SIE refers to the extent to which a company is able to successfully execute its strategy and achieve its desired outcomes. Chien and Tsai (2018) highlighted some factors that can influence SIE:

1. Clear communication and alignment: these are important to ensure that everyone in the organization understands the strategy, its goals, and their roles in executing it. This requires clear and consistent communication from top management, as well as alignment of incentives and performance metrics across different departments and levels of the organization.

2. Resource allocation: a key aspect of strategy implementation is the allocation of resources to support its execution. This includes financial resources, as well as human resources, technology, and infrastructure. Organizations need to ensure that they have the necessary resources to implement their strategy effectively.
3. Organizational structure and culture: the structure and culture of an organization can impact its ability to implement strategy effectively. A culture that supports innovation, collaboration, and risk-taking is more likely to facilitate successful strategy implementation.
4. Leadership and management: effective leadership is critical for ensuring that strategy is implemented effectively. Leaders need to provide clear direction, support, and resources to employees, while also monitoring progress and making necessary adjustments.
5. Monitoring and evaluation: regular monitoring and evaluation of strategy implementation is essential to ensure that progress is being made and to identify areas for improvement. This requires the use of performance metrics and feedback mechanisms to track progress and provide timely feedback.
6. Adaptability and flexibility: organizations need to be adaptable and flexible in their approach to strategy implementation. This includes the ability to respond to changes in the market or operating environment, as well as the ability to make course corrections when necessary.

Therefore, SIE is critical for achieving business success. By focusing on clear communication and alignment, resource allocation, organizational structure and culture, leadership and management, monitoring and evaluation, and adaptability and flexibility, organizations can increase the likelihood of successfully executing their strategies and achieving their desired outcomes. Figure 3.1 shows the dynamic capabilities framework being a key model

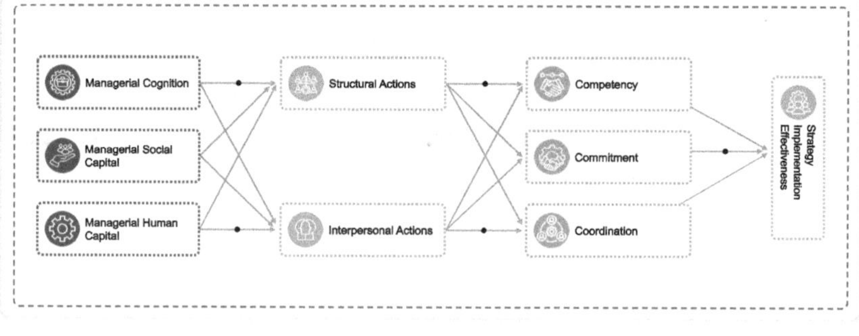

Figure 3.1 Dynamic managerial capabilities.

Source: Tawse and Tabesh (2021)

that depicts how dynamic managerial capabilities consisting of managerial cognition, managerial social capital, and managerial human capital impact managerial actions from a structural and interpersonal standpoint through key strategy implementation criteria and leading to SIE.

Managerial Actions

This highlights a broad range of factors through which managers at different levels of the organization contribute to the successful implementation of business strategies. In the extant literature, managerial actions are often referred to as "levers" (e.g., Hambrick & Cannella, 1989) or "tools" (e.g., Guth & MacMillan, 1986) that involve activities such as the arrangement of organizational structure, the application of policies, controls, and reward systems, and various forms of communication and interpersonal interaction within and across various levels of an organization. Based on the synthesis of Tawse and Tabesh (2021), managerial actions can be organized into two broad categories: structural and interpersonal (Noble, 1999).

Conditions of Effective Strategy Implementation

Building on managerial actions, the process of comparing and contrasting the factors related to SIE allowed three conditions of SI effectiveness to emerge: competence, commitment, and coordination. The conditions do not represent actions taken by managers. Instead, they represent dimensions of the emergent state that result from managerial actions and reflect three critical components required for SIE (Tawse & Tabesh, 2021). For example, managerial structural actions, such as adjustment of a compensation system, can impact SI effectiveness by improving the coordination of SI tasks (by clarifying roles and responsibilities) and by increasing commitment to carrying out those tasks.

Dynamic Managerial Capabilities

According to Tawse and Tabesh (2021), in order to better organize and understand the evidence that emerged in our synthesis regarding managerial capability, they integrated the theory of dynamic managerial capability (Helfat & Martin, 2015; Helfat & Peteraf, 2015). In general, they argued that dynamic capability theory is relevant to the SI process because it addresses a firm's ability to reconfigure its competencies (Teece et al., 1997), and "fills the gap between intention and outcome, in such a way that the outcome bears a resemblance to what was intended" (Dosi et al., 2000, p. 2). This aligns well with the definition of SI effectiveness, which is "the extent to which an organization's actions correspond to its strategic intentions" (Lee & Puranam, 2016, p. 1529). Dynamic managerial capability is an offshoot of dynamic capability theory and "helps to explain the relationship between the quality of managerial decisions, strategic change, and organizational performance" (Helfat & Martin, 2015, p. 1281). DMC theory is germane to SI because it addresses the process of organizational reconfiguration and helps explain why some firms develop the conditions of SI more effectively than others. DMC theory places the focus of dynamic capability on managers at different levels of the organization who have control over the managerial actions of SI and are responsible for the success or failure of implementation efforts (e.g., Greer et al., 2017; Hambrick & Cannella, 1989; Hrebiniak, 2006; Nutt, 1986).

Resource-Based Approach (Resource-Based View-RBV)

The resource-based approach (RBV) is a strategic management framework that emphasizes the importance of a firm's internal resources and capabilities in shaping its strategy and performance. According to the RBV, a firm's success depends on its ability to leverage its unique resources and capabilities to create a sustainable competitive advantage.

The RBV has been widely studied and applied in various industries and has generated a significant body of research and literature. According to Barney (1991), the characteristics and principles of the RBV are the following:

1. Firm-specific resources and capabilities: the RBV highlights the importance of unique, firm-specific resources and capabilities that are difficult to imitate or replicate by competitors. These resources can include physical assets, human capital, brand reputation, and intellectual property, as well as intangible capabilities such as organizational Culture and knowledge management systems.
2. Resource heterogeneity and immobility: the RBV emphasizes the importance of resource heterogeneity, or the variability and diversity of resources across firms and industries. It also highlights the immobility of certain resources, meaning that they cannot be easily transferred or acquired by competitors. This can create barriers to imitation and increase the potential for sustained competitive advantage.
3. Value, rarity, inimitability, and organization (VRIO) framework: the VRIO framework is a tool used to assess a firm's resources and capabilities in terms of their potential for creating sustained competitive advantage. The framework asks four questions: does the resource provide value? Is it rare? Is it difficult to imitate? Is the firm organized to exploit the resource?
4. Dynamic capabilities: the RBV emphasizes the importance of dynamic capabilities, or a firm's ability to adapt and respond to changing market conditions and environmental factors. This includes the ability to

identify and exploit new resources and capabilities, as well as to reconfigure existing ones in response to changing needs and opportunities.

Barney (1991) argues that a firm's resources and capabilities are the primary sources of sustained competitive advantage. He outlines the VRIO framework and emphasizes the importance of resource heterogeneity and immobility in creating barriers to imitation.

Grant (1991) applies the RBV framework to the field of strategic management, emphasizing the importance of internal resources and capabilities in shaping a firm's competitive position. He argues that the RBV can help firms identify their core competencies and develop strategies that leverage their unique strengths.

Teece et al. (1997) introduce the concept of dynamic capabilities, emphasizing the importance of a firm's ability to adapt and respond to changing market conditions and environmental factors. They argue that dynamic capabilities are key to sustaining competitive advantage over time.

Amit and Schoemaker (1993) examine the concept of organizational rent, or the value created by a firm's unique resources and capabilities. They argue that firms can capture this rent through a combination of strategic asset investment and efficient resource deployment.

According to Mandhani (2010), the RBV is an analysis and interpretation of the internal resources of organizations and emphasizes resources and capabilities needed in formulating strategy to achieve sustainable competitive advantages. According to the literature, the RBV of the organization takes an 'inside-out' view or firm-specific perspective as to how organizations create competitive advantages. Resources that are valuable, rare, inimitable, and non-substitutable (Barney, 1991) make it possible for businesses to develop and maintain competitive advantages, to utilize these resources and competitive advantages for superior performance (Collis & Montgomery, 1995; Grant, 1991; Wernerfelt, 1984).

According to Wu et al. (2010), based on the assumption of heterogeneous resources across firms, RBV emphasizes the organizational capabilities that underlie a firm's ability to excel in achieving its competitive priorities (Coates & McDermott, 2002). Critical to this is a firm's unique combination of resources and organizational capabilities. The potential for competitive advantage is related to the extent to which they are valuable, rare, inimitable, and non-substitutable (Dierickx & Cool, 1989; Barney, 1991, 1995).

Market-Based View (MBV)

The literature defines MBV as a competitive strategy which is attained as a result of the positioning of the firm in its markets and thus is often known as the ***market positioning view***. This is in contrast to the RBV which focuses on the distinctive nature of the resources and capabilities that are required to underpin and produce competitive advantage. MBV is a strategic management framework that emphasizes the importance of external market conditions and competitive forces in shaping a firm's strategy and performance. According to MBV, a firm's success depends on its ability to understand and respond to the needs and preferences of its customers, as well as to the actions and strategies of competitors in the marketplace.

The MBV framework has been widely studied and applied in various industries and has generated a significant body of research and literature. Day (1994) argues that firms need to develop a set of strategic capabilities that enable them to respond effectively to changing market conditions and customer needs. These capabilities include customer knowledge, competitor intelligence, cross-functional coordination, and resource flexibility. Day (1994) emphasizes the importance of continuous learning and adaptation in the face of dynamic market conditions.

Porter's (1996) influential article outlines the importance of competitive positioning and differentiation in achieving long-term success in the marketplace. Porter argues that a firm's strategy should be based on a deep understanding of its customers, competitors, and industry structure, and should be focused on creating a unique value proposition that sets it apart from rivals.

Golder and Tellis (2004) explore the dynamics of product life cycles and the role of market feedback and competition in shaping the trajectory of new products. They argue that early market success can create positive feedback loops that lead to rapid growth and market dominance, while later entrants face increasing competitive barriers and diminishing returns. Henderson and Cockburn (1996) apply the MBV framework to the pharmaceutical industry, examining the factors that drive innovation and research productivity. They find that firms with larger market shares and broader product portfolios are more likely to generate innovative breakthroughs and benefit from knowledge spillovers across different areas of research.

Teece (2010) argues that the MBV framework needs to be complemented with an understanding of a firm's underlying business model, which defines its value proposition, revenue streams, and cost structure. He emphasizes the importance of dynamic capabilities and strategic agility in adapting to changing market conditions and leveraging new opportunities for innovation and growth.

According to the MBV perspective, firms are considered to be fairly homogenous, and the driving forces for market competition are the branding and positioning efforts of competing firms. Further, according to MBV, identifying alternative markets as characterized by Michael Porter's five forces model is a major strategic issue. MBV does not take into account whether a firm is in position to exploit an available market opportunity, that is, whether firms have enough resource and capabilities to compete in the market place.

The Construct of the Market-Based View, Resource-Based Approach (RBV), and Organizational Capabilities

As markets are dynamic, firms' resources also need to change over a period of time to make them relevant to the changing market conditions. This perspective is based on the dynamic capabilities and is an outcome of RBV (Teece et al., 1997). Dynamic capabilities have been defined as a firm's processes that use resources: specifically the processes to integrate, reconfigure, gain, and release resources.

In assessing the interplay between the MBV, the RBV, and dynamic capabilities, it is critical to highlight that the literature suggests operational capabilities to be particularly relevant to internal resources and capabilities are the foundation for a firm's strategy; they are the primary source of profit and provide a stable basis for defining a firm's identity (Colotta et al., 2003).

While RBV primarily concentrates on types of resources and capabilities for its strategic importance, the Dynamic Capability concentrates on how these resources and capabilities need to change or update over a period of time to keep their relevance in the changing marketplace. As highlighted by Mandhani (2010), the MBV, RBV and dynamic capabilities perspective all focus on a different unit of analysis (market and firm) as well as varying degree of change (static and dynamic) as shown in Figure 3.2.

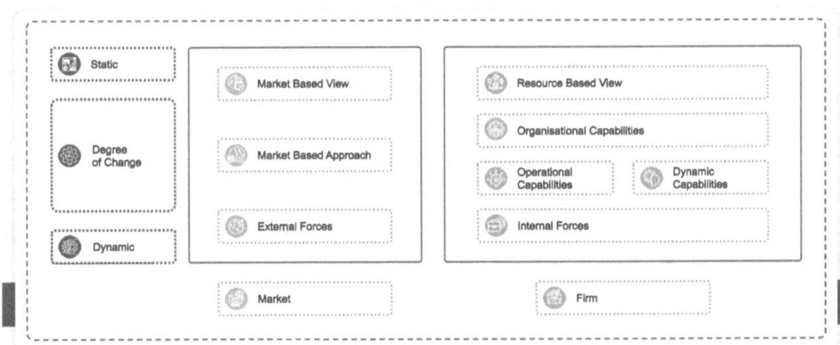

Figure 3.2 Overview of Interaction Between MBV, RBV and Organizational Capabilities.
Source: Author, modified from Mandhani (2010)

Drivers of Organizational Capabilities in Organizations

Organizational capabilities may be seen as the impetus or catalyst that enable the transformation of technical competencies into valuable results. Mckelvie and Davidsson (2009) opine that capabilities are the ability for firms to co-ordinate and deploy resources in order to achieve an organization's goal.

Building on this, we see that capabilities develop based on path dependence (including previous knowledge and resource bases of the firm), learning, and substantial time and investment into the endeavor (Ethiraj et al., 2005; Zollo & Winter, 2002).

Organizational capabilities would range from legacy themes like leadership and strategy to Kaplan & Norton's organizational design and processes within the Balanced Scorecard (Kaplan & Norton, 1992). This further includes Nohria et al. (2003), who indicate four critical primary practices (Strategy, Execution, Culture and Structure) as well as another four critical secondary practices (Talent, Leadership, Innovation and Mergers/Partnerships) which successful organizations execute exceptionally within themselves.

From an organizational standpoint, these are all critical capabilities required to drive the right organizational momentum. Further to this, and in more recent times in his new model, tagged 'the evolutionary bridge', re-emphasizes the most critical building blocks of organizational capabilities which were Learning, Change, Innovation, Collaboration, Agility, and Engagement.

Change consists of both resilience and responsiveness to events coupled with the ability to progress and adapt in a dynamic environment (Auburn, 2016). Innovation enables the conversion of both learning and change into enabling value growth for the organization. Collaboration accelerates innovation via critical focus on interdependence, whilst Agility is the ability to synchronize all four together in adaptive and responsive open or virtual business models that remain ahead of the external dynamism. Engagement is the human piece of this framework that completes the puzzle, alluding to the need to be authentic, emotional, and relational.

To summarize content from the above literary exploration, organizational capabilities are tacit, path dependent, firm specific, empirically validated capabilities which emerge gradually over time and may be influenced by an organization's history (decisions made). Furthermore, the existing literature shows that these organizational capabilities may be seen as an umbrella construct in which both Operational and dynamic capabilities fall under which we will now review.

Katrina's Kitchen

Let's take the story of "Katrina's Kitchen", a small but beloved restaurant, to illustrate the concepts of MBV, RBV, and dynamic capabilities in a more relatable way.

Katrina's Kitchen was well-known for its cozy ambiance and traditional dishes. Katrina, the owner, always kept an eye on the dining trends in her city. When she noticed a growing interest in healthy eating, she decided to introduce a range of organic and vegetarian options. This move was inspired by the MBV approach, focusing on external market conditions to find competitive advantages. Katrina understood that to succeed, her restaurant needed to align with the market's demands.

However, Katrina was aware that simply following market trends wouldn't be enough. Her restaurant had its own strengths – a skilled culinary team led by Katrina herself, a secret family recipe for the best homemade pasta in town, and a loyal customer base that valued authentic dining experiences. These unique resources and capabilities were Katrina's focus, aligning with the RBV strategy. She knew these internal strengths provided a solid foundation for her restaurant's identity and success.

As the market continued to evolve, with new dietary trends emerging and competition increasing, Katrina recognized the need for her restaurant to adapt. She introduced gluten-free pasta options and started sourcing ingredients from local organic farms. These changes required Katrina to rethink her supply chain, train her kitchen staff in new cooking techniques, and even reconfigure her menu design. This ability to adapt and reconfigure her resources demonstrated Katrina's Kitchen's dynamic capabilities – ensuring the restaurant remained relevant and competitive in a changing marketplace.

At the core of Katrina's strategy were her operational capabilities. The efficiency of her kitchen, the quality of customer service, and the ambiance of her restaurant all played critical roles. These operational strengths were not just the foundation of her day-to-day success but were pivotal in implementing changes that aligned with her MBV and RBV strategies.

They allowed Katrina's Kitchen to not just survive but thrive by effectively responding to market trends while staying true to its unique strengths.

In the story of Katrina's Kitchen, we see a practical illustration of how MBV, RBV, and dynamic capabilities work together in the real world. Katrina's ability to navigate her restaurant's strategy through understanding the market, leveraging her unique resources, and adapting to change showcases the essence of these business concepts in action.

Operational Capabilities

Operational (also known as Functional) capabilities can be defined as firm-specific sets of skills, processes, and routines, developed within the operations management system that are regularly used in solving its problems through configuring its operational resources (Wu et al., 2010).

Helfat et al. (2007) defined operational capability as the capacity of an organization to purposefully bundle its resource base in ways that enable the organization to perform the ongoing task of transforming inputs into outputs. The terms "capacity" and "purposefully" imply that managers make a choice about how best to leverage capabilities to align with a specific service objective (Coltman & Devinney, 2013).

Drivers of Operational Capabilities

Take a pause. Now, travel through your brain. Deep down. Now, tell me. How good an operational driver are you? Let us read on.

Management researchers have long been intrigued by RBV and its potential implications for operations strategy, particularly the concept of organizational capabilities. The RBV "introverted orientation" (Pandza et al., 2003) enables it to "emphasize the strategic importance of operations.

According to Wu et al. (2010), operational capabilities are particularly challenging to measure, because they emerge gradually and are tacit, embedded, and manifested differently across firms. However, operations strategy research has focused primarily on defining operational capabilities or on prescribing how they should be built. Although the strategic management literature focuses primarily on paths to competitive advantage, there has been less research related to processes that enable coordination/integration, learning, and reconfiguration (Teece, 2007) which lie squarely in the domain of operations management (Mosey, 2005). Operations management researchers have found the application of organizational capabilities construct to operations strategy a challenging academic endeavor.

While this is undoubtedly of value, academics are less willing to confront those attributes of RBV that make the perspective less operational – such as the idiosyncrasy, path dependency and context dependency of a capability.

They recognize the dynamics of capacity accumulation, yet do not explore it (Pandza et al., 2003, p. 823). We believe that the concept of organizational capabilities is directly relevant to operations strategy. For example, resources form a plant's foundation, consisting of the plant's capacity and all its stocks (Wang & Ahmed, 2007). In contrast, operational practices such as just in time (JIT) are fairly standardized activities, programs, or procedures that have been developed to address the attainment of specific operational goals or objectives (Flynn et al., 1995). Operational capabilities encapsulate both explicit elements (e.g., resources, practices) and tacit elements (e.g., know-how, skill sets, leadership) for handling a variety of problems or dealing with uncertainty. That is, operational capabilities draw on resources and operational practices to generate outcomes consistent with desired results, helping a plant develop solutions that make sense.

Dynamic Capabilities

Have you ever wondered how you can become a genius by unraveling the dynamism in your capabilities? So here is the thrill.

Before we delve into dynamic capabilities, let's break down the academic jargon here and put it in plain English. According to the Cambridge Dictionary (2019), when we say something is "dynamic", we mean it's always changing or developing, kind of like a force that keeps things moving. Now when we talk about "capabilities", we're basically referring to a company's knack for using its assets – whether they're physical stuff or intangible skills – to get things done and improve performance. It's like the special skills a company has that you can't just buy off the shelf (Amit & Schoemaker, 1993; Grant, 1991; Teece et al., 1997; Maritan & Peteraf, 2007).

Now let's put these together and talk about "dynamic capabilities", which refer to a company's ability to adapt and change over time, kind of like how senior management makes decisions based on what's happening around them. This helps the company stay fit for its environment and, when needed, tweak its existing resources or even develop new skills to tackle whatever challenges or opportunities come its way (Eisenhardt & Martin, 2000; Helfat & Peteraf, 2003; Teece et al., 1997; Winter, 2003).

Have you ever participated in a successful decision making process? How fulfilled did you feel?

Drivers of Dynamic Capabilities

In order for firms to nurture the ability to achieve new and innovative forms of competitive advantage given path dependencies coupled with market positions; Teece et al. (1997) posited that such firms would need to possess dynamic capabilities.

Accordingly, dynamic capabilities have been indicated as a firm's ability to integrate, build, and reconfigure internal and external competences to address rapidly changing environments (Teece et al., 1997). This is consistent with earlier definitions of dynamic capabilities as the subset of competences/capabilities which allows the firm to create new products and processes and respond to changing market circumstances (Teece & Pisano, 1994).

Expanding further, Concepta (2012) opined that dynamic capabilities act as a buffer between firms' resources and the shifting business environment by helping a firm adjust its resource base and thereby maintain the sustainability of its competitive advantage, which otherwise might be eroded.

Dynamic capabilities have also been reported to be the organizational and strategic routines by which firms achieve new resource configurations as markets emerge, collide, split, evolve and die (Eisenhardt & Martin, 2000). For Wang and Ahmed (2007), dynamic capabilities can be regarded as a firm's behavioral orientation which is to constantly integrate, reconfigure, renew, and recreate its resources and capabilities, as well as upgrade and reconstruct its core capabilities in response.

Distilling these definitions, in more recent years several researchers such as Helfat et al. (2007, p. 4) defined dynamic capabilities as

> the capacity of an organization to purposefully create, extend, and modify its resource base comprising of the tangible, intangible, and human assets (or resources) as well as capabilities which the organization owns, controls, or has access to on a preferential basis.
>
> (Helfat et al., 2007)

In this reasoning, we can transpose dynamic capabilities versus the operational capabilities, which is driven by the RBV and focuses on the selection of the most apt and appropriate existing skill set to deliver organizational objectives. The dynamic capabilities view focuses on resource development and renewal.

Concepta (2012) rightly posited therefore that organizational capabilities can be thought of as marketing skills, distribution skills, product development skills, organization skills, and so on. They are general capabilities that potentially are applicable to different industries. They represent the ways that people and resources are brought together to accomplish the organizational mission, vision, and priorities

Dynamic Capabilities – Process or Mechanism/Operation

Maritan and Peteraf (2007) emphasized that the effectiveness of dynamic capabilities depends on the underlying organizational and managerial processes. They suggested that understanding dynamic capabilities requires delving into the surrounding processes, considering it both a process and a mechanism. Eisenhardt and Martin (2000) supported this idea, highlighting that dynamic capabilities are often viewed as processes due to their performance being contingent on the underlying processes.

Maritan (2001) proposed that testing and validating dynamic capabilities can also aid in refining them. Senior Management plays a crucial role in aligning organizational objectives with the deployment and refinement of dynamic capabilities. Exploitation, as described by March (1991), involves refining existing competencies and technologies for predictable returns, while agility requires balancing resilience and quick adaptation with strategic experimentation (Ireland et al., 2003; Sheffi & Rice, 2005; Röder et al., 2014).

Without deliberate efforts from organizational leaders to adjust intra- and extra-organizational systems in response to environmental changes, achieving a balance between ambidexterity and agility remains challenging (Doz & Kosonen, 2010; Bucherer et al., 2012). This balance involves managing conflicts between short-term gains and long-term investments, as well as between individual and collective organizational knowledge (March, 1991).

Organizational Traps

According to Tushman and O' Reilly III (2013b) and McGrath (2013), there are certain organizational traps which militate against the implementation of OA by organizations. Table 3.1 highlights these traps and includes the researchers' perspectives on the same.

Whilst it's critical to understand the inherent traps organizations face that act as barriers to implementing ambidexterity, on closer inspection we may explore how firms that intentionally approach ambidexterity face the perennial problem of the dichotomy that exists between exploitative and explorative aspects of OA.

Exploration may be associated with searching, variation, risk taking, experimentation, play, flexibility, discovery, innovation whilst exploitation can be seen as refinement, choice, production, efficiency, selection, implementation and execution (March, 1991). Raisch and Birkinshaw (2008) opined that creating an equilibrium between both exploratory and exploitative OA is critical to organizational success. This is consistent with an earlier school of thought which implies that this adaptive process benefits from the interplay of exploration of new possibilities/frontiers and exploitation of old certainties/legacies (March, 1991).

Converging into a corroborative line of thought, we may adopt the prisoner's dilemma as an analogous representation (Holland, 1992). Consistent with the March's (1991) postulation – exploration and exploitation (being

Table 3.1 The Various Organizational Traps

Organizational Traps	*Key Concepts*	*Main Authors*
Success Trap	The intoxication of prior success which then creates a false paradigm of perpetual success	(Brazen, 2019)
First mover Trap	The notion that being the first mover in an industry affords the firm ongoing sovereign power and/or dominance in that industry	(Tushman & O'Reilly III, 2013a)
Superiority Trap	Continuous improvement is the backbone of sustainability for any firm in today's world.	(McGrath, 2013)
Quality Trap	The tendency to deliver service levels above which the customer is willing to pay for	(McGrath, 2013)
Hostage-resources Trap	The notion that militates against exploring new frontiers because top executives are focused on driving existing profitable businesses	(McGrath, 2013)
White-space Trap	When opportunities are a misfit to the company's overall strategy and thus need to be discarded	(McGrath, 2013)
Empire-building Trap	The belief that the more asset heavy an organization is, the better- this leads to bureaucracy	(McGrath, 2013)
Sporadic Movement Trap	This connotes the non-institutionalization of innovation as a system versus a quick fix	(McGrath, 2013)
Strategy Trap	The adoption of a fixed strategy and the belief that strategy cannot be changed regardless of market dynamics	(Kim & Mauborgne, 2005)
Cultural Inertia Trap	The cultural bias towards a certain work/organizational fit which may militate against sustainability in the market place	(Perrow, 1986)

Source: Adapted from McGrath (2013), Tushman and O' Reilly III (2013b)

the players) can either compete or cooperate to achieve success (freedom). According to the prisoner's dilemma the most favorable solution for both players (exploration and exploitation) would be a 'co-operate' scenario versus a 'compete' scenario. By cooperating, both players would achieve the most optimum outcome as shown in Table 3.2.

However, more recent studies carried out by Fujimoto and Kaneko (2019) reveal a highly structured differential and integral analysis of the prisoner's dilemma which extends the learning and by extension, lends reality to the interplay between exploitation and exploration.

Based on the above, repeated game enables better understanding of the situation by both players (exploitative and explorative). Based on this, and forging ahead – sequential cooperation (i.e., always choosing CC) is more

Table 3.2 Exploration – Exploration via the Prisoners' Dilemma

Choice	*Exploration Co-operate*	*Exploration Compete*
Exploitation cooperate	Superior return (30/30)	Exploration benefits (0/50)
Exploitation complete	Exploitation benefits (50/0)	Normal return (10/10)

Source: Adapted from Holland, 1992, p. 71, and cited by Nguyen (2014)

beneficial than reciprocal defection and cooperation (i.e., repeatedly alternating between CD and DC).

Fujimoto and Kaneko (2019) therefore postulated that the exploitative relationship is stabilized by both the exploiting and exploited players. The exploiting player receives a higher payoff than the other player does and often receives a higher payoff than that under the pure CC. The exploited player receives a lower payoff than the other player does but secures at least the minimax payoff, which is obtained under the pure DD. This lends weight to the understanding that it's critical to have a simultaneous dose of both exploitation and exploration, but one may 'cannibalize' the other, which altogether may still lead to a better outcome enabling organizational transformation.

Synergizing the Background Logic of Dynamic Capabilities Across Several Authors

To converge the various perspectives of authors on dynamic capabilities, Peteraf (2009) highlighted the background logic of various authors in articulating the chain of flow of the elements of dynamic capabilities. As posited by Peteraf (2009) and highlighted in Table 3.2, Logic I by Teece (1997) shows that dynamic capabilities have prior paths (firm history, previous investments) leading to current firm positions (tangible and intangible assets), consistent with evolutionary economics. Logic II by Eisenhardt and Martin (2000) shares an almost consistent logic with this. But Logic III with Teece (2007) focuses on particular types of dynamic capabilities, using a chain of logic that expands upon that in Teece et al. (1997) and including dynamic capabilities investment leading to a series of re-configuration of same capabilities which would ultimately improve firm performance. Teece (2007) specifically calls this the dynamic capability of opportunity identification ('sensing') and investment in these opportunities ('seizing') which leads to new positions and paths, which then affects firm performance in terms of growth, profits and competitive advantage.

Based on all these, the researcher synthesized all three logics into logic IV showing dynamic capabilities being observed more from a contextual approach. From this approach, senior management champions the cause of building resources and capabilities, which then enable the organization to

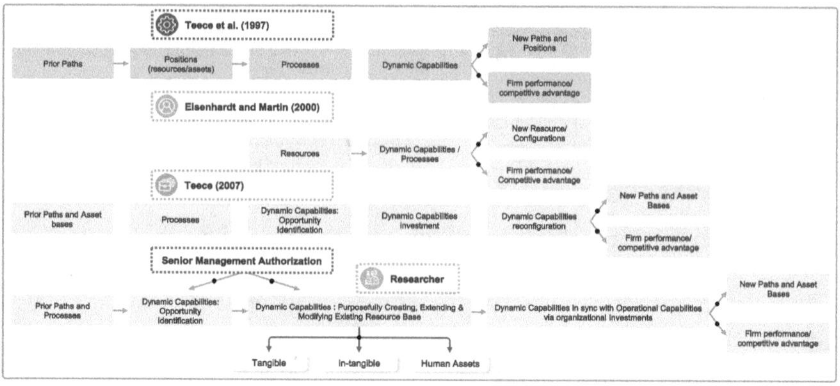

Figure 3.3 Synergizing the Background Logic of Dynamic Capabilities Across Several Authors.
Source: Author

purposefully create, extend and modify the organization's existing resource base from a tangible, intangible and human asset standpoint to deliver a cycle of reconfigured capabilities which ensure consistent firm performance in terms of growths, profits and competitive advantage.

Conclusion

The comprehensive exploration of OA as a strategy in Chapter 3 underscores the significance of practical frameworks, theoretical foundations, and the interplay of various strategic management perspectives in enabling organizations to navigate the complexities of OA implementation.

The chapter emphasizes the importance of assessing and enhancing OA maturity through models like OAMM and SIE while highlighting the synergies between market-based and resource-based approaches. The narrative of Katrina's Kitchen serves as a powerful illustration of how the convergence of these perspectives, coupled with the cultivation of dynamic capabilities, can enable organizations to thrive amidst change.

However, the chapter also cautions against the pitfalls of organizational traps that can hinder OA implementation, emphasizing the need for vigilance and proactivity in identifying and overcoming these barriers. By synthesizing the background logic of dynamic capabilities across several authors, the chapter provides a nuanced understanding of how these capabilities can be developed and harnessed to drive organizational performance.

As the chapter concludes, it becomes evident that the strategic underpinnings of OA lay the groundwork for a deeper exploration of the drivers and enablers of ambidexterity. Among these critical factors, organizational culture emerges as a pivotal element in shaping an organization's ability to balance exploration and exploitation.

Chapter 5 will unpack the intricate relationship between OA and culture, drawing upon seminal works and practical illustrations to illuminate the role of culture in fostering an ambidextrous mindset and navigating the challenges of dynamic environments.

4 Organizational Ambidexterity and Organizational Culture

Introduction

Building upon the strategic foundations of OA explored in the previous chapter, Chapter 4 delves into the intricate relationship between ambidexterity and organizational culture. The chapter emphasizes the critical role of culture in shaping an organization's ability to balance exploration and exploitation, recognizing that the successful implementation of OA strategies hinges on the alignment of cultural values, beliefs, and practices with ambidextrous objectives.

The chapter introduces the concept of organizational culture, its drivers, and the dimensions that define it, drawing upon the seminal works of scholars such as Kotter, Heskett, Schein, Cameron, and Quinn. By examining the various facets of culture, the chapter provides a comprehensive understanding of how an ambidextrous organizational culture can be cultivated to foster the underlying values, beliefs, and principles necessary for achieving ambidexterity.

Furthermore, the chapter introduces the Competing Values Framework (CVF) as a powerful tool for assessing and understanding the different types of organizational culture and their implications for ambidexterity. The engaging narrative of "Tech & Taste" serves as a practical illustration of how the alignment of culture and capabilities can enable businesses to thrive in the face of change.

By building upon the strategic insights from the previous chapter and delving into the cultural dimensions of ambidexterity, Chapter 4 sets the stage for a deeper exploration of organizational agility and its role in navigating turbulent markets. The chapter highlights the interplay between ambidexterity, culture, and agility, offering valuable insights for leaders seeking to build resilient and adaptable organizations in an ever-changing business landscape.

Organizational Culture

Organizational culture is a key concept in organizational theory and management. It refers to the shared values, beliefs, attitudes, and behaviors that

DOI: 10.4324/9781003488224-4

define an organization and shape how employees interact with one another and with external stakeholders. Over the years, numerous scholars have studied organizational culture from various perspectives, and a vast body of academic literature has emerged on this topic.

One of the seminal works on organizational culture is the book "Corporate Culture and Performance" by John Kotter and James Heskett (1992). In this book, the authors argue that organizational culture has a significant impact on organizational performance and that a strong culture can be a source of competitive advantage.

Another influential scholar in the field of organizational Culture is Edgar Schein. In his book "Organizational Culture and Leadership" (2010), Schein describes organizational culture as a set of shared assumptions, values, and beliefs that shape behavior in organizations. He identifies three levels of organizational culture: artifacts and behaviors, espoused values, and basic underlying assumptions. Schein argues that understanding the basic underlying assumptions of an organization's culture is essential for managing organizational change.

Other scholars have approached organizational culture from different angles. For example, Cameron and Quinn (2011) developed the Competing Values Framework, which identifies four types of organizational culture: clan, adhocracy, market, and hierarchy. Deal and Kennedy (1982) proposed the "strong culture" hypothesis, which suggests that a strong, cohesive culture can improve organizational performance. Meanwhile, O'Reilly and Chatman (1996) argue that organizational culture is shaped by the socialization process, through which new employees learn and internalize the values and norms of the organization.

Overall, the literature on organizational culture is vast and diverse, with various theoretical frameworks and perspectives. However, there is a general consensus that organizational culture is a critical factor in organizational success and that it is worth understanding and managing in a deliberate and intentional way.

Organizational culture and ambidexterity are two key concepts in organizational theory and management. Organizational culture refers to the shared values, beliefs, attitudes, and behaviors that define an organization and shape how employees interact with one another and with external stakeholders.

Research has shown that organizational culture can have a significant impact on an organization's ability to achieve ambidexterity. For example, Zacher and Wilden (2014) found that a strong culture of innovation was positively related to exploration activities, while a strong culture of efficiency was negatively related to exploration activities. This suggests that organizations with a strong culture of innovation may be better able to balance exploration and exploitation activities.

Another study by Raisch and Birkinshaw (2008) found that the degree of OA is influenced by the alignment between the organizational culture and the ambidextrous strategy. Specifically, they found that organizations that emphasize both efficiency and innovation in their culture are more likely to achieve ambidexterity.

In addition, some studies have suggested that specific cultural traits may facilitate ambidexterity. For example, Gupta and Krishnan (2009) found that a culture of experimentation (i.e., a willingness to take risks and learn from failure) was positively related to both exploration and exploitation activities.

These studies suggest that organizational culture plays a critical role in facilitating or hindering OA. A strong culture of innovation and a willingness to take risks and experiment may help organizations to achieve a balance between exploration and exploitation activities and to adapt to changing environments. On the other hand, a culture that emphasizes efficiency and stability may hinder an organization's ability to explore new opportunities and adapt to changing conditions.

Drivers of Organizational Culture

Organizational culture is shaped by a variety of internal and external factors that influence employee behavior and decision-making. These factors, known as drivers, can have a significant impact on the type of culture that emerges within an organization. Understanding the drivers of organizational culture is essential for organizations seeking to create a culture that aligns with their goals and objectives.

Founders and leaders play a critical role in shaping organizational culture. They establish the values and beliefs that guide behavior and set the tone for the organization. The history of the organization can also influence its culture, as employees draw on past experiences and traditions to guide their behavior. The industry and external environment in which the organization operates can also shape its culture, with different industries and external environments favoring different cultural characteristics.

Effective management of organizational culture requires a deep understanding of the drivers that influence it. Organizations that are intentional about shaping and managing their culture can create a positive and productive workplace that supports their goals and objectives. By understanding the drivers of organizational culture, organizations can create a culture that aligns with their mission, vision, and values, and that supports the development of desired attitudes and behaviors among employee.

Organizational culture is shaped by a variety of internal and external factors. Here are some common drivers of organizational culture according to Zacher and Wilden (2014):

1. Founders and leaders: founders and top leaders play a crucial role in shaping the culture of an organization. They often set the tone for the organization and establish the values and beliefs that guide behavior.

2. Organizational history: the history of an organization can influence its culture, as employees may draw on past experiences and traditions to guide their behavior and decision-making.
3. Industry and external environment: the industry and external environment in which an organization operates can also shape its culture. For example, organizations in highly competitive industries may have a more aggressive and competitive culture, while those in more collaborative industries may have a more cooperative and collaborative culture.
4. Organizational size and structure: the size and structure of an organization can also affect its culture. Larger organizations may have more formal and bureaucratic cultures, while smaller organizations may have more flexible and informal cultures.
5. Employee diversity: the diversity of employees within an organization can influence its culture. A diverse workforce can bring different perspectives and values to the organization, which can shape its culture.
6. Organizational values and beliefs: the values and beliefs that an organization holds can also shape its culture. For example, an organization that values innovation and risk-taking may have a more dynamic and entrepreneurial culture, while an organization that values stability and predictability may have a more conservative and risk-averse culture.

Therefore, organizational culture is shaped by a variety of factors, including the founders and leaders, organizational history, external environment, organizational size and structure, employee diversity, and organizational values and beliefs. Understanding these drivers can help organizations to intentionally shape and manage their culture in a way that supports their goals and objectives.

Schein (2010) opined that organizational culture is both a dynamic phenomenon and a function of organizational dimensional factors. We may assume therefore that organizational culture is a key input factor in both the hard and soft constituents of the organization's overall business environment being driven by both the behavioral parts of the organizational context, as well as the structural components represented by processes and systems (Wang & Rafiq, 2014). Therefore, besides exploring the context behind a firm´s activity system which represents the current business model and the basis for the business model changes, one must further take into account the underlying cognitive foundations and logic that drive these activities (Hock et al., 2015).

This school of thought drawing on organizational culture literature reveals that parts of the capabilities that enable business model innovation are determined by the firm´s underlying organizational Culture. Hock et al. (2015) distilled the underlying organizational values of the two main business model design themes (novelty and efficiency) and linked these to the firm's capabilities that foster business model innovation to infer that novelty-oriented values foster capabilities in favor of business model innovation, while efficiency-oriented values do not show positive effects.

Ambidextrous Organizational Culture

Wang and Rafiq (2014) state that organizational culture when viewed through the lens of ambidexterity displays the underlying values, beliefs, and principles that act as a foundation for an organization's management system coupled with the set of management practices and behaviors that articulate these principles. Denison (1996) argues that organizational Culture constitutes the informal, behavioral part of organizational context and as such complements the formal, structural component (e.g. processes and systems). Wang and Rafiq (2014) further buttressed this concept by revealing the four (4) traits inherent in organizational culture: (a) perceived involvement and participation on the part of organizational members; (b) adaptability in response to external conditions without abandoning one's underlying character; (c) normative integration and consistency; and (d) a mission combining economic and noneconomic objectives; mission and consistency ensure stability and direction, while adaptability and involvement allow change and flexibility (Denison & Mishra, 1995).

Behind this, Schein (1990) opined that organizational culture develops contiguously alongside the organization's ability to cope with the dual problems of direction and flexibility as well as external adaptation and internal integration. The duality of organizational culture alongside the process of organizational learning then forms the basis of the conceptualization of ambidextrous organizational culture.

Dimensions of Organizational Culture

Cameron and Quinn (1999), who investigated the contribution of developed organizational culture on organizational effectiveness and organizational success, advised that organizational culture may be observed in four different types being hierarchy, market, clan and adhocracy.

Types of Organizational Culture

The four organizational culture types were mapped out by Cameron and Quinn (1999) based on the Competing Values Framework (CVF) model as seen in Figure 4.1.

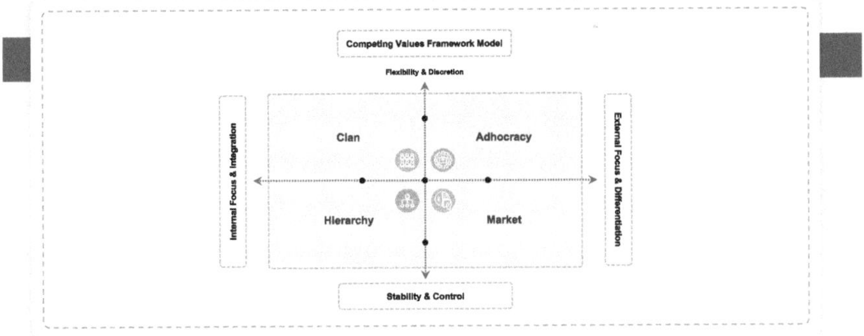

Figure 4.1 Competing Values Framework (CVF) Model Mapping Out Organizational Culture Types.

Source: Cameron and Quinn (2006)

Clan (Collaborative) Culture

This is developed when organizations are more skewed towards the internal chassis of the company and therefore value the responsiveness of employees above other external stakeholders. According to Cameron and Quinn (1999), the boundaries of this organizational culture is shaped between organization focus and flexibility/dynamism.

In this construct, one would evidently notice a family like nexus holding the organizational as one unit and prioritizing the needs of the organization above the needs of the customer as far as it's not a make-or-break company decision.

Hierarchy (Control) Culture

The Hierarchical organizational culture is located between internal organization focus/integration and stability/control boundaries. As posited by Cameron and Quinn (1999), this is an organizational culture type where the leadership is effective because it is in nature mechanical and bureaucratic. Overall, we see that hierarchies bring structure and rigor to operations through controlled operating processes as they ensure that things are executed per organizational objectives.

Market (Competitive) Culture

Similar to the balanced phenomenon we see with the hierarchy culture; we have the Market (competing) organizational culture. Here, Cameron and Quinn (1999) remarked that employees in these culture types are success-oriented due to the fact that they lend importance to personal interests rather than organizational goals and emphasize on the concepts of planning, performance and efficiency.

Due to the external landscape focus, market organizational cultures are often competitive leveraging on the needs delivered and at same time continue to win in the marketplace. Following this is a slight tendency to compromise on responsiveness and nurturing of the organizations.

Adhocracy (Creative) Culture

A bit more contrary to the Clan (Collaborative) organizational culture, we have the Adhocracy (Creative) Market organizational culture which is extremely outwards looking and on the opposite side of the divide versus the Clan Culture. As posited by Cameron and Quinn (1999); this organizational culture with its external-oriented and dynamic structure refers to the culture of an organization in entrepreneurial, flexible, innovative and creative areas.

Adhocracy organizational culture thrives where organizations are outward looking and focused on being agile and responsive establishing an environment where organizations value pace of work, innovation and risk taking to remain super agile in meeting external customer needs.

According to Hamed et al. (2018), although the CVF is labeled competing because the criteria within the model seem conflicting opposites at first, the originators of the framework recognize that the criteria are neither mutually exclusive nor necessarily orthogonal (Schmiedel & Brocke, 2012). In reality, it may be possible for organizations to take on all four perspectives simultaneously.

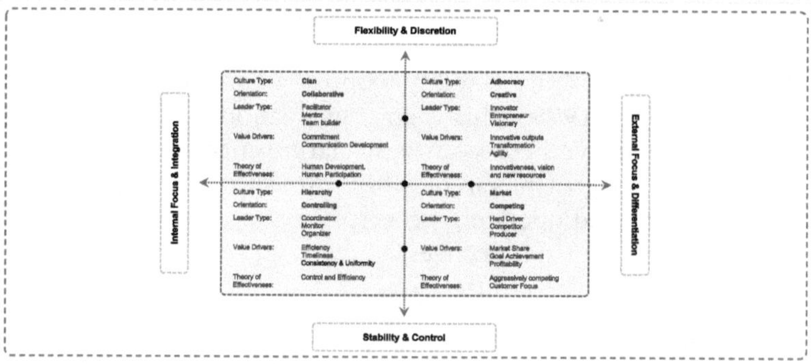

Figure 4.2 Competing Values of Leadership, Effectiveness and Organizational Theory.
Source: Cameron and Quinn (2006)

Tech & Taste

Let's meet Alex, the owner of "Tech & Taste", a company that's as unique as its name suggests. Alex's venture began in the heart of the city, where the love for technology and good food intersected. "Tech & Taste" isn't just a café that serves delicious meals and the best coffee in town; it's also a hub for tech enthusiasts and startups. Here, innovation is as much a part of the menu as the espresso.

Building the Culture

From the beginning, Alex knew that the secret sauce to success was more than just great food or the latest gadgets – it was about creating a culture that supported both. Like Schein described, Alex saw culture as something living, something that had to keep up with the buzzing energy of the café. This culture became the backbone of "Tech & Taste", influencing how the team worked and how customers engaged with the space. It was about being dynamic and having the ability to shift gears from the aroma of coffee to the buzz of brainstorming sessions.

"Tech & Taste" is always on the move, much like the market it thrives in. Alex believes in the power of dynamic capabilities, ensuring that the café can reconfigure its resources, whether it's rearranging the space to host meetups or training the staff in the latest tech trends to help customers. This agility has made "Tech & Taste" a local landmark that stays relevant and continues to grow its loyal following.

Wang and Rafiq's perspective on ambidextrous culture resonated with Alex. "Tech & Taste" is a place that blends the best of both worlds – solid, dependable operations, and a willingness to take calculated risks. It's the harmony between serving that consistently perfect cup of coffee (Hierarchy Culture) and jumping on the latest tech wave (Adhocracy Culture).

At "Tech & Taste", everyone's like family. The staff knows not only your order by heart but also your latest project or tech challenge. This Clan Culture ensures that while the company looks inward, making sure the team feels valued, it never loses sight of the customer experience.

Cameron and Quinn's Competing Values Framework (CVF) isn't just a theory at "Tech & Taste"; it's lived daily. Alex and the team balance the need for control (Hierarchy) with the push for competition (Market Culture), without sacrificing the creativity that's at the heart of their business (Adhocracy). And throughout it all, they ensure that the warm, collaborative spirit (Clan) is what customers feel every time they walk through the doors.

"Tech & Taste" is more than a café or a tech space – it's a microcosm of a thriving culture that understands the value of blending tradition with

innovation, stability with flexibility, all while brewing up a storm of continuous growth and success. Alex's story shows that when culture and capabilities align, businesses can not only survive but become cornerstones of their community.

Organizational Agility

According to the literature, organizational agility is defined as the capacity to flexibly respond to changes in the environment by quickly adjusting product and service offerings, and is increasingly becoming critical to achieving sustained competitive advantage (Singh et al., 2013). Exploring more views, Dove (1999) opined that organizational agility is the ability of an organization to thrive in a continuously changing, unpredictable business environment. To that effect, the current descriptions of organizational agility encompass (i) a firm's ability to detect and "respond quickly, timely and with dexterity to proactive and reactive needs of change" (Röder et al., 2014, p. 3) (ii) with a view to enabling an organization to thrive in a turbulent and competitive environment (Goldman & Nagel, 1993; Dove, 1999, 2002; Vazquez-Bustelo et al., 2007).

We may assess organizational agility across various fronts. Portfolio agility refers to the capacity to shift resources quickly and effectively between business areas to leverage inherent scale (Baskarad & Koronious, 2018). Strategic agility connotes the ability to sense strategically relevant information from the entire organization, seize emerging opportunities and burst company boundaries.

Furthermore, Baskarad and Koronious (2018) helped to reveal the differentiation between resource agility, which deals with the access to necessary human and technological resources, from process agility which deals with the flexibility of the core processes, and linkage agility as relative to the nature of stakeholder interaction.

Doz and Kosonen (2008) define strategic agility as the capacity to continuously adjust and adapt strategic direction in a core business to create value for a company. Weber and Tarba (2014) have defined it as "the ability to remain flexible in the face of new developments". Concurrently, Teece et al. (2016) refer to agility as the capacity of an organization to redeploy/redirect its resources efficiently and effectively to value creating and value protecting (and capturing) higher-yield activities as warranted by internal and external circumstances.

In addition to managing Stigler's demand shocks, agile organizations must manage supply-side uncertainty and adjust strategy as necessary and desirable. Agility is costly to develop and maintain and sometimes even more costly if it is non-existent. Moreover, agility is not a one-size-fits-all solution. Costs vary according to the structures and systems in place. Issues arise as to how it is best achieved. In one case, it might make sense to maintain redundancy or slack; in another, the best approach may be to build or buy general-purpose equipment or diversify the firm's customer base. Firms can sometimes buffer themselves against risk by using financial instruments, thereby potentially obviating the need to enable agility through the firm's asset base. Importantly, the capabilities required to respond to negative events are often different from those needed to take advantage of positive developments. Agility requirements are thus context sensitive. In stable markets, for example, it may be profitable to optimize basic operations and achieve efficiency at the expense of agility because the cost of protecting against possible future disruption may be too large to justify sacrificing current profits. However, when there is deep uncertainty, agility is likely to be a valuable organizational attribute with the caveat that is in the hands of good managers.

Operational agility is positioned as the ability to "exploit both revenue-enhancing and cost-cutting opportunities within the core business more quickly, effectively, and consistently than rivals do" (Sull, 2010, p. 6). Thus, operational agility correlates with ambidexterity exploitation. Christensen (1997) argued that while weakly managed organizations stumble because of "bureaucracy, arrogance, tired executive blood, poor planning, short-term investment horizons as well as inadequate skills and resources", it is not only these organizations that stumble in the face of market and technological change and disruption (p.7). He argued that even well-managed giants that have their "competitive antennae up, listen astutely to their customers and invest aggressively in new technologies", still stumble and lose market dominance (Christensen, 1997, p. 7). It thus begs the question, why?

There have been multiple answers to this question, starting with Christensen (1997) himself citing what he termed "The innovator's dilemma" (p. 9). Christensen's "innovator's dilemma" basically states that the logical decisions and practices taken by management, previously critical to the success of organizations, are also often the reasons why these organizations lose their market leadership positions when faced with disruptive technological change (Christensen, 1997, p. 9). While most well-managed organizations excel at "sustaining technologies that improve the performance of their products" to their customer's satisfaction, "disruptive technologies change the value proposition in a market" (Christensen, 1997, p. 175). Thus, decision-making and resource-allocation processes previously key to the success of established organizations, within the first context, are the very processes that reject disruptive technologies when the context changes (Christensen, 1997, p. 86). Given that in turbulent markets market prediction is rendered ineffectual, operational agility requires an organizational mindset, systems and processes for continuous self-disruption. Organizations, therefore, need to put in place systems for continuous exploration, dissemination of information and solutions explored and a systematic construction of processes to "translate corporate priorities into focused action" (Christensen, 1997; Sull, 2010, p. 6). In agreement, McGrath (2013) posits that for a continuous creation of transient advantages, organizations must reconfigure their advantages, keeping the existing source of competitive advantage "fresh" as more and more competitors enter the fray, and to ultimately disengage and replace, moving on in a timely and strategic fashion before the original advantage is completely eroded (Leavy, 2004, p. 4).

To conclude, Sull (2010) advocates for prudent and agile business diversification, describing this as portfolio agility. Sull (2010) asserts that without portfolio agility, seasoned executives, when faced with the decision to protect established businesses or invest in portfolio choices for new risky bets, will choose to protect established businesses. The risk to the business is redundancy and death in the face of technological disruption (Christensen, 1997). Therefore, to effectively enable portfolio agility, Sull (2010) argues for the cultivation of versatile general managers who can dynamically move from business to business, cultivating both exploitation and exploration of new and old through diversification when required.

Organizational agility has consistently been put forth as the dynamic capability upon which competitive advantage rests (Ireland et al., 2003; Sheffi & Rice, 2005; Gupta et al., 2006). At opposite ends of the spectrum of Organizational agility are the concepts of entrepreneurial agility and adaptive agility. Entrepreneurial agility concerns itself with functions of seeking and identifying new opportunities followed by the proper planning and execution of the opportunities (Ireland et al., 2003) while adaptive agility deals with organizational resilience and adaptation to "environmental change in order to maintain competitive parity and leadership" (Röder et al., 2014, p. 3). Adaptive agility concerns itself with functions that enable the organization to cope with uncertainty and recover quickly to disruption "without fundamentally changing products or processes" (Röder et al., 2014, p. 3).

Christensen (1997) identified two types of innovations that organizations can engage in: disruptive innovation and sustaining innovation. Disruptive innovation is the kind of innovation that leads to new markets and new business models (Christensen, 1997; Ireland et al., 2003). This is the kind of innovation more closely aligned to the notion of entrepreneurship (Ireland et al., 2003), and as such, entrepreneurial agility. Sustaining innovation is incremental innovation implemented through improvement and refinement cycles (Christensen et al., 2002). This is the kind of innovation that enables organizational adaptation and resilience and is more aligned to adaptive agility (Sheffi & Rice, 2005; Röder et al., 2014).

While they sit on opposite ends of the spectrum, adaptive and entrepreneurial agility are two different but very effective organizational capabilities to anticipate, plan for and respond to market disruption. The agility component of both concepts highlights and enforces that the response must be executed in the quickest and swiftest manner, permitting a quick time to market while the opportunity is still within its lifetime (Sambamurthy et al., 2007).

The competitive arena in business environments has changed in many ways behind globalization of markets, rapid technological change, shortening of product life cycles, and the increasing aggressiveness of competitors, requiring that they respond flexibly and rapidly to stay in the game (Jansen, 2005). Whilst organizations are beginning to affirm this, the execution of this revamped strategy within the most tailored framework still haunts organizations and this is the organizational woe that this research is designed to address.

Ambidexterity has been viewed from numerous frameworks: 'sequential' meaning transitioning structures overtime to align with firm's strategy; 'Structural' depicting a more simultaneous framework involving structural fits of exploratory and exploitative constructs; and 'Contextual' where individuals own the transition between the explorative and exploitative divide (Tushman & O'Reilly III, 2013a). Whilst all these frameworks are largely valid in theory, a more pragmatic way to navigate through ambidexterity as a system would be through the framework of dynamic capabilities (Tushman & O'Reilly III, 2013a).

Several schools of thought have given life to the context of dynamic capabilities. Decades ago, the dynamic capabilities approach was said to provide a coherent framework which can both integrate existing conceptual and empirical knowledge and facilitate prescription (Teece & Pisano, 1994). In the later years, Teece et al. (1997) (as cited by Tushman & O'Reilly III, 2013b) defined dynamic capabilities as "the firm's ability to integrate, build, and reconfigure internal and external competencies to address rapidly changing environments". In more recent years, we see dynamic capabilities explained as the capacity of an organization to purposefully create, extend, or modify its resource base (Helfat et al., 2007, p. 1, as cited by Tushman & O'Reilly III, 2013a).

Key to note here is the involvement of senior leadership in ensuring dynamic capabilities is the active conductor through which the organization can transmit its OA leading to catalyzed organizational transformation. It would be safe to therefore state that OA (sequential, simultaneous, or contextual) is adequately conveyed on the platform of dynamic capabilities which could be concisely reflected in a complex set of decisions and routines that enable the organization to sense and seize new opportunities through the reallocation of organizational assets and consequently leading to organizational transformation (Tushman & O'Reilly III, 2013b).

Whilst the phenomenon of dynamic capabilities has been applauded as a key capability required by firms in transforming themselves and remaining relevant in the ever-evolving competitive business landscape, it's important to recognize that these capabilities can only function and remain engrained in the DNA of organizations through the platform of operational capabilities. Wu (2010) opines that operational capabilities are firm-specific sets of skills, processes, and routines, developed within the operations management system, that are regularly used in solving its problems through configuring its operational resources. Together, the interplay of dynamic and operational capabilities would afford the right organizational capabilities construct required to enable organizations transform and remain ambidextrous.

Conclusion

The examination of organizational ambidexterity and culture in Chapter 4 underscores the pivotal role of culture in fostering ambidexterity and enabling organizations to navigate the complexities of balancing exploration and exploitation. By exploring the drivers and dimensions of organizational culture, the chapter provides a nuanced understanding of how culture shapes an organization's ability to adapt and thrive in the face of change.

The Competing Values Framework (CVF) emerges as a powerful tool for assessing and understanding the different types of organizational culture, emphasizing the importance of striking a balance between competing values such as control and flexibility, internal focus and external orientation. The narrative of "Tech & Taste" serves as a compelling illustration of how the alignment of culture and capabilities, coupled with the cultivation of an ambidextrous mindset, can enable organizations to succeed in dynamic environments.

The interplay between organizational ambidexterity, culture, and agility is crucial for building resilient and adaptable organizations in the face of ever-evolving business landscapes. The insights gleaned from this chapter lay the foundation for a deeper exploration of how organizations can effectively navigate turbulent markets by leveraging the power of dynamic capabilities and organizational agility.

The subsequent chapter will delve into the complex interplay between these concepts, drawing upon the RBV and the VRIO framework to highlight the importance of unique resources and capabilities in achieving sustained competitive advantage amidst market turbulence.

5 Organizational Ambidexterity in Turbulent Markets

Introduction

Building upon the insights from the previous chapter on the interplay between organizational ambidexterity, culture, and agility, Chapter 5 delves into the complex dynamics of navigating turbulent markets. The chapter draws upon the RBV and the VRIO framework to highlight the importance of unique resources and capabilities in achieving sustained competitive advantage amidst market uncertainties.

The chapter explores the critical role of dynamic capabilities in enabling organizations to adapt and reconfigure their resources in rapidly changing environments. By examining the various facets of organizational flexibility, the chapter emphasizes the significance of an organization's ability to respond effectively to external changes.

Through the engaging narratives of Digital Dreamers and Katrina's Kitchen, the chapter illustrates how the convergence of OA, dynamic capabilities, and organizational agility can lead to exceptional organizational performance. These narratives serve as compelling examples of how organizations can strategically align their resources, capabilities, and cultural values to thrive in the face of market disruptions and technological shifts.

By building upon the cultural foundations of ambidexterity explored in the previous chapter and delving into the strategic imperatives of navigating turbulent markets, Chapter 5 sets the stage for a profound exploration of the practical implications and strategies for fostering these critical organizational attributes. The chapter aims to equip leaders with the insights and tools needed to build resilient, adaptable, and high-performing organizations in an increasingly complex and dynamic business landscape.

OA, Dynamic Capabilities, and Organizational Agility

According to the RBV, we understand that organizational resources and capabilities (which comprise both operational/functional and dynamic

DOI: 10.4324/9781003488224-5

capabilities) are ultimately key determinants of attaining a competitive advantage. Amit and Schoemaker (1993) expressed that resources are like an inventory of resource factors managed by the organization, while capabilities are inherent capacities to deploy resources usually in combination using organizational processes, to achieve desired objectives being "information-based, tangible or intangible processes that are firm-specific and are developed over time".

Based on value rarity, imitability, and organization (VRIO) analysis (an internal approach to assess an organization's level of competitive advantage) originally developed by Barney (1991) we understand that for a firm's particular organizational capability to truly constitute a competitive advantage it must scale through the four attributes hurdles, meaning the resource must be valuable, rare, imperfectly imitable, and non-substitutable. We substitute the 'organization' part of VRIO which actually depicts 'resources and capabilities which are organized to exploit' based on recommendation from Barney (1995) in his sequel study meaning the resource must be duly positioned to remained organized to capture the value of the resource. A resource or capability that meets all four requirements can bring sustained competitive advantage for the company.

Based on the above and using the VRIO concept, distinctive and superior resources and capabilities may become the basis for competitive advantage (Peteraf, 1993). Building on this, there need to be other short- and long-term limits to competition (Peteraf, 1993). However, the RBV does not seem applicable to high-velocity markets (situations of rapid and unpredictable change), for which dynamic capabilities may provide a more suitable theoretical explanation (Eisenhardt & Martin, 2000).

According to Baskarad and Koronious (2018), rather than focusing on resources as the main input factor of competitive advantage, the dynamic capabilities perspective considers those processes that allow organizations to integrate, build and reconfigure resources and capabilities to address rapidly changing environments (Teece et al., 1997; Eisenhardt & Martin, 2000). Further to this, dynamic capabilities underpin both evolutionary adaptation (Helfat et al., 2009) and entrepreneurial innovation (Teece, 2007).

The general consensus from Baskarad and Koronious (2018) is therefore that though the dynamic capabilities are an integral part of the enabling of an organization with respect to securing a sustained competitive advantage, the dynamic capabilities in themselves cannot suffice in establishing a sustained competitive advantage. In other words, they enable organizational adaptation to the environment as well as the shaping of that environment. While being important enablers, dynamic capabilities are not themselves a source of sustained competitive advantage (Eisenhardt & Martin, 2000). As such, they are a necessary, but not a sufficient, condition for sustained competitive advantage.

In positioning ambidexterity and agility as continuous dynamic capabilities to facilitate business transformation in volatile and complex environments, it is expected that the rate of change within and without the organization will require contextual decision making on the fly. This leaves very little time for transfer of knowledge should the dynamic capability sit outside of the task teams involved with the change.

In the bustling city where innovation meets tradition, two seemingly disparate ventures, Digital Dreamers and Katrina's Kitchen, embark on journeys that highlight the essence of OA, dynamic capabilities, and organizational agility, all culminating in exemplary organizational performance.

The Unlikely Synergy

Digital Dreamers, a tech startup, and Katrina's Kitchen, a traditional yet forward-thinking restaurant, might appear worlds apart at first glance, yet their stories intertwine through shared strategies of adaptation and innovation. Both ventures recognize the importance of leveraging their unique resources and capabilities, as outlined in the RBV, not just as static assets but as the foundation for dynamic growth and competitive advantage.

As the tech landscape evolves, Digital Dreamers continually reconfigures its resources, integrating the latest innovations to stay ahead of the curve. Similarly, Katrina's Kitchen adapts by sourcing local and organic ingredients and incorporating healthy, gluten-free options into its menu. These actions exemplify dynamic capabilities in motion – both ventures adeptly navigate changes in their environments, reshaping their strategies and offerings to meet new demands.

The concept of organizational ambidexterity comes to life as Digital Dreamers balances its investment in cutting-edge research (exploration) with optimizing its current software offerings (exploitation). Katrina mirrors this balance by experimenting with new culinary techniques and menu items while preserving her restaurant's cherished traditional dishes. This dual approach enables both businesses to explore new opportunities without sacrificing their core strengths, illustrating the power of ambidexterity in fostering innovation and stability.

In markets characterized by rapid and unpredictable change, agility becomes paramount. Digital Dreamers exemplifies agility by swiftly adjusting its project timelines and resource allocations in response to emerging tech trends. Katrina's Kitchen shows similar flexibility, quickly adapting to customer feedback and seasonal ingredient availability. This organizational agility allows both ventures to make informed and timely decisions that align with market needs and internal goals, driving sustained competitive advantage.

The stories of Digital Dreamers and Katrina's Kitchen converge on a critical point: the resultant organizational performance. Their strategic embrace of ambidexterity, dynamic capabilities, and agility allows them not only to navigate market turbulence but also to excel within it. Digital Dreamers emerges as a leader in its niche, while Katrina's Kitchen becomes a beloved community staple, each achieving growth, profitability, and a loyal customer base.

A Commercial Symphony

Together, Digital Dreamers and Katrina's Kitchen compose a commercial symphony that underscores the practical application and benefits of integrating OA, dynamic capabilities, and organizational agility. Their journeys reveal that success in today's business landscape requires more than just innovation or tradition alone – it demands a harmonious blend of both, guided by strategic foresight and the flexibility to adapt and thrive.

In this narrative, the fusion of Digital Dreamers' technological prowess with Katrina's culinary heritage showcases a broader lesson for businesses: that embracing complexity, fostering adaptability, and maintaining a dynamic balance between exploration and exploitation are the keystones of enduring success and outstanding organizational performance.

Organizational Flexibility

Flexibility is defined as the extent to which new and alternative decisions are generated and considered in strategic planning, allowing for positive organizational change and adaptation to environmental turbulence (Rudd et al., 2008).

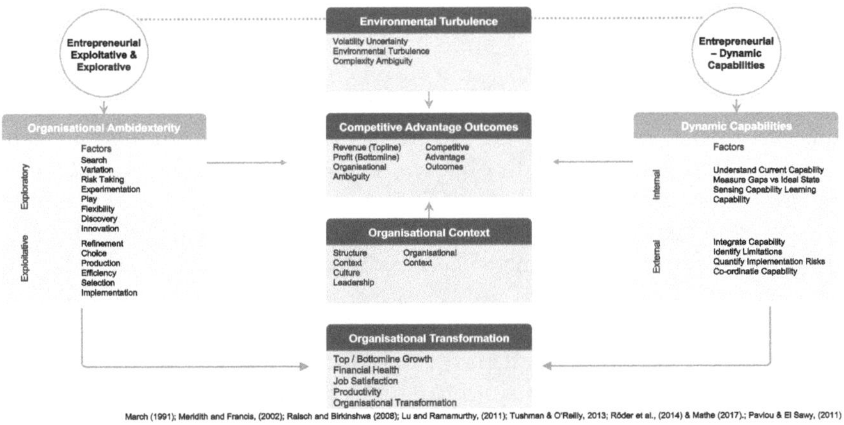

Figure 5.1 OA and Agility in Turbulent Markets.

Source: March (1991), Meredith and Francis (2002), Raisch and Birkinshaw (2008), Lu and Ramamurthy (2011), Tushman and O'Reilly III (2013b), and Röder et al. (2014)

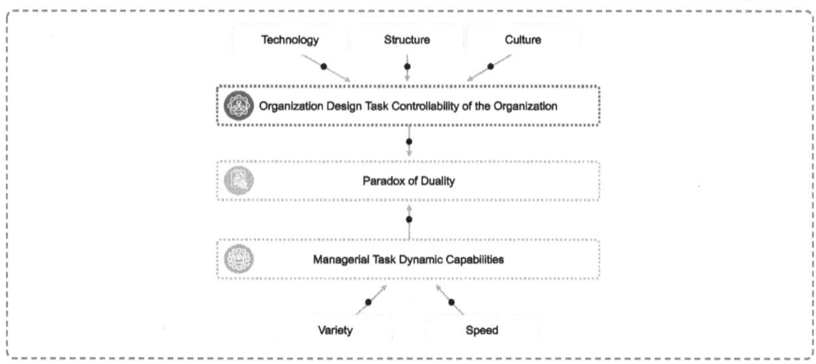

Figure 5.2 Organizational Flexibility and Associated Managerial and Organizational Design Tasks.

Source: Modified from Volberda (1996)

As opined by Volberda (1998), organizational flexibility reflects the capacity of an organization to respond to various kinds of external change. More than ever, the need for organizational flexibility has become more and more apparent behind the ever dynamic business ecosystem and the transient advantages organizations at best are able to secure in competitive markets (D'Aveni, 1994).

Types of Organizational Flexibility

According to Volberda (1996), in a turbulent environment, management needs an extensive multidimensional collection of capabilities. The dynamic capabilities that endow the firm with flexibility are manifested in four (4) types of organizational flexibilities, namely steady state, operational, structural and strategic.

To expand further, Steady State Flexibility comprises static procedures to optimize the firm's performance when level/nature of throughput is largely stable; Operational Flexibility consists of routine capabilities based on present goals/structures of the organization; Structural Flexibility comprises of managerial capabilities to adapt the organizations structure, decision and communication processes to suit changing conditions; and Strategic Flexibility entails managerial capabilities which are related to the goals of the environment or the organization (Volberda, 1996).

Table 5.1 summarizes the types of organizational flexibility at a glance.

Table 5.1 Internal and External Types of Flexibility

Types of Flexibility	*Internal*	*External*
Routine Maneuvering Capacity	Internal Operational Flexibility Variation of production volume Building up of Inventories Use of Crash teams	External Operational Flexibility Use of temporary labor Multisource reserving of capacity with suppliers
Adaptive Maneuvering Capacity	Internal Structural Flexibility Creating Multifunctional Teams Changing managerial Roles Alterations in Control Systems	External Structural Flexibility Purchasing of components from suppliers Purchasing of Sub-assemblies from suppliers Developing of subcomponents together with suppliers
Strategic Maneuvering Capacity	Internal Strategic Flexibility Dismantling of current Strategy Applying new technologies Fundamentally renewing products	External Strategic Flexibility Creating new product market combinations Using market power to defer entry and control competitors Engaging in political activities to counteract trade regulators

Source: Adapted from Volberda (1996)

Organizational Learning

According to Miller (1996), organizational learning is the knowledge acquisition made by actors (individuals and groups) when these can, and are available to, apply it in the decision-making process, or use it to influence others within the organization. organizational learning is a social phenomenon (Curado, 2014a). Each individual's learning depends upon the knowledge that other members of the organization possess (Figueiredo, 2003). As posited by Maier et al. (2003), organizational learning, being a process, will last more time than a simple event (Maier et al., 2003). Curado (2014a) posited that causal ambiguity, strongly associated to path dependency or historic dependency (the accumulation of experiences, learning, errors and successes) as it creates a reality (values, language, communication, products, technology, inter alia) with multiple and complementary origins can hardly be replicated. Organizational learning is therefore a way to build causal ambiguity (a way to make difficulties for other firms to imitate the organization) and establishing a base for competitive advantage (Lei et al., 1996).

Relating these to OA, Gupta et al. (2006), He and Wong (2004) and Baum et al. (2000), posited that learning acquired via local search, experiential refinement, and selection would be termed exploitation, while exploration would refer to learning gained through processes of concerted variation, planned experimentation and play. According to Curado (2014a), other researchers defined exploitation as the mere reuse of existing knowledge and thus assigned all instances of learning to exploration (Rosenkopf & Nerkar, 2001; Vassolo et al., 2004; Vermeulen & Barkema, 2001).

Curado (2014a) also went further to review the different classifications of organizational learning such as double-loop versus single-loop learning (Argyris & Schön, 1978); generative versus adaptive learning (Senge, 1990); local search versus long jump (Levinthal, 1997); and product innovation versus production-oriented learning (McKee, 1992).

Most scholars had applauded this 'two type organizational learning' as essential for long-term organizational success (Gupta et al., 2006; Levinthal & March, 1993; March, 1991). Conversely, March (1991) had discredited this positing that such a learning combo is fundamentally incompatible.

Theoretical Framework on OA

The below shows an aggregation of key concepts surrounding OA. The framework shown in Figures 5.3 and 5.4 builds on the work of Raisch and Birkinshaw (2008) and other existing literature already discussed and attempts to simplify into Figure 2.10 shown below.

Organizational Design

Organizational design is a process that involves shaping an organization's structure and systems to achieve its goals efficiently and effectively. According to Robbins and Judge (2017), organizational design is "the process of selecting and managing aspects of organizational structure and culture to enable the organization to achieve its goals".

Organizational design can be viewed from various perspectives, such as structural, cultural, and strategic. Structural design refers to the configuration of an organization's formal structure, including its hierarchy, roles, and communication channels (Daft, 2018). Cultural design, on the other hand, refers to the values, beliefs, and assumptions that shape an organization's behavior (Schein, 2010). Finally, strategic design concerns the alignment of an organization's structure and culture with its strategic goals and external environment (Galbraith, 2014).

There are several approaches to organizational design, such as the contingency approach, the systems approach, and the socio-technical approach (Robbins & Judge, 2017). The contingency approach emphasizes that there is no one best way to design an organization, and the design should be contingent on the organization's context and environment (Burns & Stalker, 1961). The systems approach views an organization as a complex system of interrelated parts that work together to achieve common goals (Katz & Kahn, 1966). The socio-technical approach emphasizes the importance of designing an organization's technology and social systems together to optimize productivity and employee satisfaction (Trist & Bamforth, 1951).

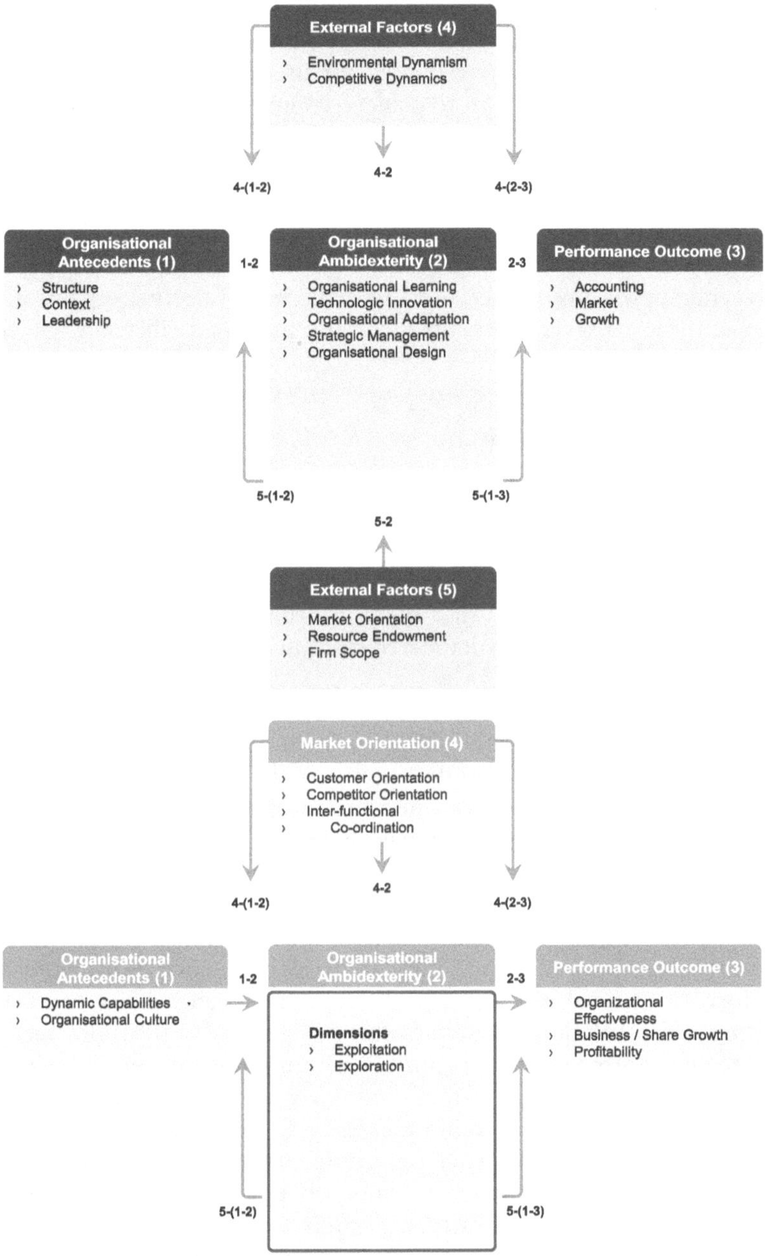

Figure 5.3 & 5.4 Overview of OA Framework.

Source: Raisch and Birkinshaw (2008)

Organizational design has several benefits, including increased efficiency, effectiveness, and adaptability (Robbins & Judge, 2017). Efficient organizational design ensures that resources are used optimally, while effective design enables an organization to achieve its goals. An adaptable organizational design allows an organization to respond to changes in its environment quickly.

Nonetheless, organizational design is a crucial process that involves shaping an organization's structure and culture to achieve its goals efficiently and effectively. Organizational design can be viewed from various perspectives, and several approaches can be used to achieve it. Effective organizational design can lead to several benefits including increased efficiency, effectiveness, and adaptability.

Organizational Design and OA

Organizational design and OA are two concepts that are closely related. OA refers to an organization's ability to simultaneously exploit its existing resources and capabilities while exploring new opportunities for growth and innovation (Tushman & O'Reilly, 2007). This ability requires a specific type of organizational design that allows for the coexistence of two distinct modes of operation: the exploitation of existing capabilities and the exploration of new opportunities.

Incorporating innovation into organizational design requires the concept of ambidexterity, which was first introduced by Duncan (1976). March (1991) theorizes that ambidexterity is the fight for scarce resources of the entire organization, which must be allocated between explorative and exploitative activities. Ambidexterity is defined as "simultaneously pursuing both incremental and discontinuous innovation from hosting multiple contradictory structures, processes, and cultures within the same firm" (Tushman & O'Reilly, 1996). The allocation of resources toward one extreme of the ambidextrous continuum hinders the performance of the other one. Therefore, firms need to excel at both exploration and exploitation while balancing and combining the two to stay competitive in the long run.

To achieve ambidexterity, a number of ambidexterity types have been proposed with the two most established types being structural and contextual ambidexterity. Structural ambidexterity involves utilizing the organizational design of firms to provide a unit(s) for exploration and units for exploitation, allowing firms to simultaneously pursue both incremental and discontinuous innovation. Contextual ambidexterity, on the other hand, allows individuals to allocate their time between exploration and exploitation based on their own judgments, by setting appropriate programs to achieve alignment and adaptability across an entire business-unit (Gupta et al., 2006).

Another approach to balancing exploration and exploitation is sequential ambidexterity, which proposes reorienting organizational structures over time to adapt to environmental shifts. This approach allows firms to change their course between long periods of exploitation and short periods of exploration, but requires significant resources and can be challenging for large firms due to organizational inflexibilities inherent in large organizations (Tushman & Romanelli, 1985a).

The exploitation of existing capabilities is typically associated with the optimization of current products, processes, and services. This mode of operation is characterized by a focus on efficiency, reliability, and incremental improvements. On the other hand, the exploration of new opportunities involves experimenting with new ideas, technologies, and business models. This mode of operation is characterized by a high degree of uncertainty, risk-taking, and experimentation.

OA requires a specific type of organizational design that allows for the coexistence of these two modes of operation. One approach to achieving this is through structural ambidexterity, where an organization creates separate structures or units to focus on exploitation and exploration (Gibson & Birkinshaw, 2004). Another approach is contextual ambidexterity, where an organization creates a shared culture and strategic framework that allows for the simultaneous pursuit of exploitation and exploration (O'Reilly & Tushman, 2013).

Organizational design plays a crucial role in enabling OA. A well-designed organization can facilitate the coexistence of exploitation and exploration by creating the necessary structures, processes, and culture to support both modes of operation. However, achieving OA is not easy, and organizations must carefully balance the trade-offs between exploitation and exploration to ensure long-term success (Levinthal & March, 1993).

Drivers of Organizational Design

Organizational design is influenced by various internal and external factors, which can be classified as drivers of organizational design. These drivers include the organization's strategy, size, technology, environment, culture, and leadership.

First, an organization's strategy plays a crucial role in determining its organizational design. The design must be aligned with the organization's strategic goals and objectives. For example, if an organization's strategy is to innovate, then it may adopt a more flexible and decentralized structure to encourage creativity and experimentation (Gibson & Birkinshaw, 2004).

Second, an organization's size also affects its design. As an organization grows in size, it may need to restructure to maintain efficiency and effectiveness. For example, a small start-up may have a flat and informal structure, while a large MNC may have a more hierarchical and formal structure (Tushman & O'Reilly, 1996).

Third, technology is another driver of organizational design. The design must be tailored to the technology that an organization uses to ensure that it operates efficiently. For example, an organization that relies heavily on technology may have a flatter structure that promotes teamwork and collaboration (Gupta et al., 2006).

Fourth, the environment in which an organization operates also influences its design. The external environment can be turbulent and unpredictable, which may require the organization to be more adaptable (Gupta et al., 2006).

Organizational Learning

Organizational learning is a process by which an organization acquires knowledge, skills, and capabilities that enable it to adapt and improve over time. Organizational learning has been defined in different ways by different scholars. One of the most common definitions is that of Argyris and Schön (1978), who describe it as "the detection and correction of error" in an organization's behavior. Other scholars have described organizational learning as the process of acquiring and using knowledge, skills, and capabilities to improve organizational performance and achieve competitive advantage. Organizational learning is a complex and ongoing process that requires continuous effort and attention from an organization's leadership and employees.

Conceptual Refinement

Calibration

In order to "sense check" literature review findings (main concepts and important issues) with those working strategically in modern organizations, the researcher conducted informal data collection with senior manager in different industries. While a systematic and detailed literature review was conducted and led to the conceptual model presented in Figure 1.1, it was important to ensure that in such a dynamic and fast-moving area a precise and parsimonious approach was adopted prior to embarking on data gathering; to explore the main concepts, the proposed relationships, and general face validity of the model drawn from the literature, and to "sense check", to use a more colloquial term.

Informal Interviews

The researcher investigated via his interviews with key managers and business leaders, the impact of rapidly changing [high velocity] business environments on organizations and furthermore their organization's ability to navigate through the turbulence.

Based on informal interview sessions conducted with ten (10) working professionals across various industry/country/function combinations the researcher was able to explore the relevance of concepts explored during literature review as well as responses from industry experts. Concepts explored were as below:

1) Organizational Ambidexterity
2) Organizational Culture
3) Operational Capabilities
4) Adaptive Agility
5) Dynamic Capabilities
6) Innovation
7) Organizational Flexibility
8) Flexibility
9) Organizational Adaptability
10) Adaptive Agility
11) Organizational Agility
12) Open Communication

Following this, the researcher proceeded to validate the same themes confirmed by professionals in Phase one but this time with another set of professionals. Additionally, professionals were asked four (4) questions aimed at understanding the importance, criticality and perception of these themes. The questions are detailed in Appendix II (Part I).

As shown below, OC and DC are depicted to have the highest level of importance when assessing variables enabling organizations transform.

Having reviewed the literature on key concepts surrounding ambidexterity and impacts as well as moderators of ambidexterity on overall organizational performance along with what industry practitioners had to say about this, the researcher converged key concepts to explore within the study.

These concepts included the following: OA, dynamic capabilities and organizational culture.

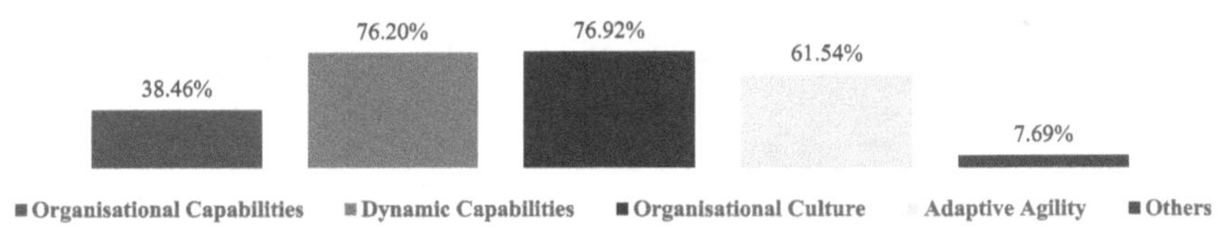

Figure 5.5 Importance Factors enabling Organisations transform

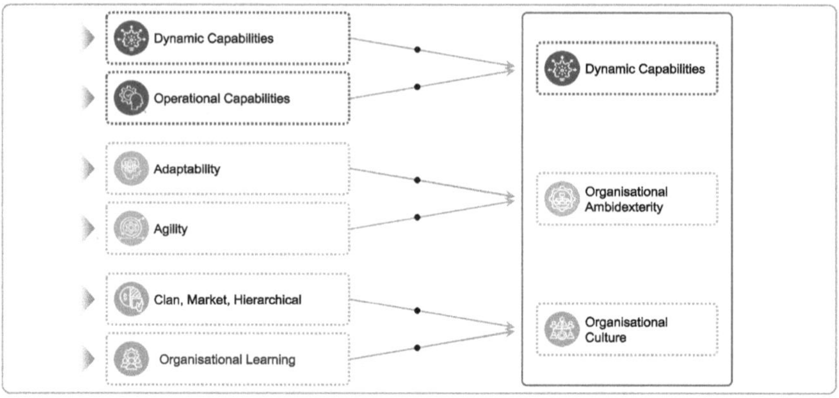

Figure 5.6 Convergence Based on Validation of Themes With Industry Practitioners

With this, the researcher went back to extant literature to understand more about how these concepts tie up together and how they influence and affect organizational performance. Raisch and Birkinshaw (2008) have previously designed a conceptual model that gathered the drivers (antecedents) and moderators (via external factors), and these impact the organizations performance. However, with feedback from industry professionals, the researcher then revised the model to a leaner version expressed in the components below:

1) The drivers of OA as dynamic capabilities and organizational culture as per industry leaders' feedback.
2) The concept of OA comprising the components:
   a) Exploration.
   b) Exploitation.
   c) Adaptability.
   d) Agility, as captured in extant literature between Raisch and Birkinshaw (2008) and Peng et al. (2019).
3) The external influencing factors or 'moderators' in the form of market orientation, and comprising inter-functional co-ordination, customer, and competitor as further expressed in the extant literature (Peng et al., 2019).

Conclusion

The examination of OA, dynamic capabilities, and organizational agility in navigating turbulent markets in Chapter 5 underscores the critical importance of these concepts in achieving sustained competitive advantage amidst uncertainty and change. By grounding the discussion in the RBV and the VRIO framework, the chapter highlights the significance of unique resources and capabilities in driving organizational performance.

The narratives of Digital Dreamers and Katrina's Kitchen serve as powerful illustrations of how the strategic alignment of ambidexterity, dynamic capabilities, and agility can enable organizations to thrive in the face of market disruptions and technological shifts. The chapter also emphasizes the role of organizational flexibility, both internally and externally, in effectively responding to the ever-evolving business landscape.

As the chapter concludes, it becomes evident that the interplay between OA, dynamic capabilities, and organizational agility is crucial for building resilient and adaptable organizations in turbulent markets. The insights gleaned from this chapter lay the foundation for a comprehensive discussion and analysis of a study exploring the relationship between OA and firm performance.

The subsequent chapter will delve into the implications of the study's findings, drawing upon both qualitative and quantitative approaches to provide a nuanced understanding of the factors influencing OA implementation and its impact on organizational performance.

6 Integrated Discussion and Overview

Introduction

Building upon the insights from the previous chapter on the critical role of OA, dynamic capabilities, and organizational agility in navigating turbulent markets, Chapter 6 presents an integrated discussion and overview of a study exploring the relationship between OA and firm performance. The chapter utilizes both qualitative and quantitative approaches to analyze OA implementation, key barriers and drivers, variations in exploration and exploitation across industries, and differences in managerial perspectives between low- and high-performing organizations.

By delving into the implications of the study's findings and addressing each research question, the chapter provides valuable insights for practitioners seeking to enhance their organization's performance through effective OA implementation. The discussion highlights the complex nature of OA implementation, involving factors such as organizational culture, leadership, and resources.

Furthermore, the chapter introduces a diagnostic tool developed using artificial intelligence/machine learning (AI/ML] to assess OA levels and recommend actions for improvement. By examining the theoretical contributions to the RBV and MBV and the practical implications for organizations, this chapter offers a comprehensive analysis of the study's findings.

The integrated discussion and overview presented in Chapter 6 serve to synthesize the key takeaways from the previous chapters, providing a holistic perspective on the relationship between OA and firm performance. By bridging theory and practice, the chapter aims to equip leaders and managers with the knowledge and tools necessary to foster an effective managerial and organizational implementation of ambidexterity in their pursuit of sustained success in today's dynamic business environment.

DOI: 10.4324/9781003488224-6

Discussion and Implications of Organizational Ambidexterity and Firm Performance

The analysis found a significant and positive relationship between OA and firm performance (O'Reilly & Tushman, 2004a; Javalgi & White, 2011). This is in line with previous studies (Chen & Miller, 2011) that have found that organizations that effectively balance both exploration and exploitation activities are more likely to achieve long-term success and improved performance outcomes.

Moreover, the findings also suggest that OAI is a complex process that involves multiple factors (Zahra & George, 2002), including organizational Culture (Choi & Lee, 2009), leadership (Chen & Miller, 2011), and resources (Liu et al., 2018). Organizations that effectively address these factors are more likely to successfully implement ambidexterity and achieve improved performance outcomes (Zahra & George, 2002).

In terms of limitations, the results should be interpreted with caution given the limitations of the sample size, data sources, and research design used in the study (Creswell, 2014). Further research may be necessary to confirm the results and to provide a more comprehensive understanding of the relationship between OA and firm performance (Yin, 2014).

In conclusion, the findings of the study highlight the importance of OAI for organizations and provide practical implications for organizations seeking to improve their performance (O'Reilly & Tushman, 2004b). The results suggest that organizations that effectively implement OA are likely to see improved performance outcomes (Javalgi & White, 2011), and that effective implementation requires a strategic and comprehensive approach that takes into account multiple factors (Zahra & George, 2002).

Discussion and Implications of Managerial Decisions in Embedding of OA

This study suggest that managerial decisions and actions play a crucial role in the implementation and embedding of OA in organizations. Both qualitative and quantitative results indicate that the support and commitment of top management, as well as clear communication and allocation of resources, are key drivers for the successful implementation of OA. On the other hand, resistance to change, lack of resources, and conflicting priorities are significant barriers to OAI.

Qualitative findings highlight the importance of a supportive organizational culture that encourages innovation and risk-taking, as well as a clear understanding of the strategic importance of OA. This can be achieved through active involvement of top management in the implementation process, clear communication of the benefits of OA, and allocation of resources to support OA initiatives.

Quantitative results suggest that the implementation of OA is positively related to firm performance. The results indicate that firms that adopt a more balanced approach to exploration and exploitation activities are likely to achieve higher performance levels. Additionally, the results suggest that managerial decisions and actions that support OAI can positively influence firm performance.

In conclusion, the findings of this study suggest that managerial decisions and actions play a critical role in the implementation and embedding of OA in organizations. By understanding the drivers and barriers to OAI, managers can take practical steps to enhance the effectiveness of their OA initiatives.

Discussion, Barriers, and Implications of OA in Practice

The findings of the study on the key barriers and drivers to implementing OA in practice have important implications for organizations and practitioners. These findings can be used to inform strategies for overcoming the barriers and leveraging the drivers to effectively implement OA.

The results suggest that one of the main barriers to OAI is a lack of senior management support and buy-in. In this case, organizations may need to focus on educating and communicating the benefits of OA to senior management and other stakeholders to secure their support. Additionally, the results indicated that limited resources, such as time and budget constraints, are also a barrier to OAI. In this case, organizations need to allocate sufficient resources to support the implementation process and ensure its success.

On the other hand, the results indicated that a supportive organizational culture and clear strategic vision are key drivers of OAI. In this case, organizations need to focus on creating a culture that values innovation and experimentation, and aligning their OA strategy with their overall business strategy.

Discussion and Implications of Market Conditions, Resource Availability, and Organizational Culture

The implementation of exploration and exploitation varies across industries, and this has significant implications for a firm's OA and performance. The findings of this study, based on both qualitative and quantitative approaches, provided valuable insights into the factors that influence the implementation of exploration and exploitation in different industries.

From the qualitative results, the study found that factors such as market conditions, resource availability, and organizational culture play a crucial role in determining the level of exploration and exploitation in different industries. For example, in industries with high levels of competition and rapidly changing market conditions, firms need to focus more on exploration activities to stay ahead of their competitors. In contrast, firms in industries with more stable market conditions place a higher emphasis on exploitation activities.

The quantitative results of the study provide further insights into the relationship between the implementation of exploration and exploitation and organizational performance. The findings suggest that firms that are able to effectively balance their focus on both exploration and exploitation are more likely to achieve higher levels of performance. This highlights the importance of OA for firms across different industries.

In conclusion, the implications and discussion of the findings of this study suggest that the implementation of exploration and exploitation can vary significantly across industries. The results of the study can provide valuable insights into the factors that influence the implementation of OA and highlight the importance of balancing exploration and exploitation for firms to achieve higher levels of performance.

The implications and discussion of the findings of this study suggest that the implementation of exploration and exploitation can vary significantly across industries. The results of the study can provide valuable insights into the factors that influence the implementation of OA and highlight the importance of balancing exploration and exploitation for firms to achieve higher levels of performance. O'Reilly and Tushman (2004a) provided a comprehensive overview of the concept of OA and the importance of balancing exploration and exploitation activities for firms to achieve higher levels of performance. Teece (2010) provided insights into the relationships between business models, business strategy, and innovation, and how these factors can influence the implementation of OA in different industries. Pisano (2006) provided a comprehensive analysis of the role of collaboration, competition, and corporate culture in the development of innovation and the implementation of OA in organizations.

Incremental Implications of the Study

Supportive Structure for OA Implementation

One of the key findings is that a supportive organizational culture is crucial for the successful implementation of OA. A culture that values exploration and innovation as well as efficiency and effectiveness can provide the necessary support for balancing exploration and exploitation. For example, a study by Anderson et al. (2016) found that organizations with a culture that values experimentation and risk-taking are more likely to successfully implement ambidexterity.

On the other hand, a culture that prioritizes efficiency and stability over exploration and innovation can act as a barrier to ambidexterity implementation. A study by Li et al. (2018) found that organizations with a strong emphasis on control and stability may struggle to balance exploration and exploitation, as they may not have the necessary cultural support for risk-taking and innovation.

Additionally, it is important to note that cultural change is not a one-time event, but rather a continuous process. A study by O'Reilly and Tushman (2004b) found that organizations must continuously evolve their culture in order to maintain ambidexterity, as the needs and challenges of the organization may change over time.

OA Diagnostic Tool

Developing a diagnostic tool to assess OA provided valuable insights into the strengths and weaknesses of a company's culture and helped identify areas for improvement. The key components of OA, such as adaptability, alignment, coordinating capability, integrating capability, learning capability, sensing capability, diversity, customer orientation, competitor orientation, and inter-function coordination, were identified. The tool was designed using the outcome of the quantitative study.

Based on the results of the assessment, recommendations for improvement can be made. For example, if the company is lacking in adaptability, it may be recommended that they establish a more flexible structure and encourage innovation and risk-taking. If the company is not well-aligned, it may be recommended that they create a clear mission statement and develop a shared understanding of their goals.

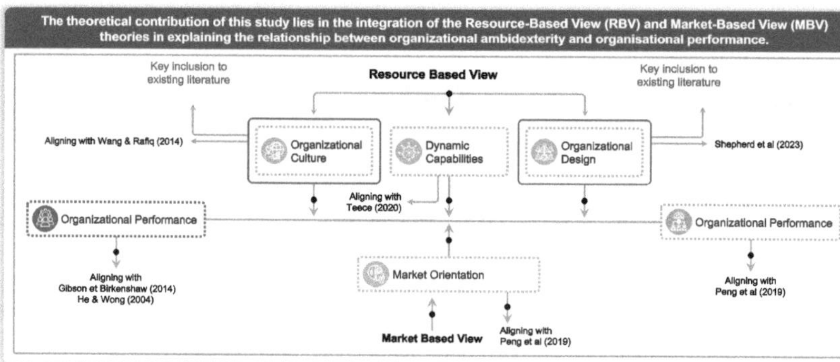

Figure 6.1 Contribution to Theory: Final Conceptual Framework on OA

It's important to note that improving OA requires a holistic approach and should involve a wide range of stakeholders within the organization, including management, employees, and customers.

In conclusion, a diagnostic tool for assessing OA can provide valuable insights into an organization's culture and help identify areas for improvement. However, it's essential to approach OA improvement holistically and involve all relevant stakeholders in the process.

Theoretical Contribution

The theoretical contribution of this study lies in the integration of the RBV and MBV theories in explaining the relationship between OA and performance. The study provides empirical evidence for the role of organizational culture, dynamic capabilities, market orientation and organizational design as drivers of OA and its impact on performance. The findings contribute to the existing literature on OA by showing how a combination of RBV and MBV theories can be used to understand the factors that contribute to successful implementation of OA and its impact on organizational performance. This provides a comprehensive understanding of the relationship between these variables and can be used to inform future research and practice in the field.

The study made several theoretical contributions to the field of OA research.

First, the study contributed to the RBV and Market-Based MBV by examining the role of dynamic capabilities and market orientation in the implementation of OA. This integration of both RBV and MBV provides a more comprehensive understanding of the relationships between these variables and OA, and further validates the findings from the qualitative phase. Additionally, the dynamic capabilities framework (DCF) provides a useful lens through which to view OAI (Teece et al., 1997). The DCF emphasizes the importance of firms' ability to reconfigure their resources and capabilities in response to changing environments, and OA can be seen as a key component of these dynamic capabilities.

Furthermore, the Market Orientation (MO) concept also informs the conceptual framework of OA and its impact on performance (Narver & Slater, 1990). A market-oriented firm is characterized by a strong focus on customers and competitors, and OA can be seen as a way for firms to respond to changes in the market and improve their performance.

Additionally, the study's integration of organizational culture and design into the model contributes to the understanding of how these variables can support the implementation of OA. From the RBV, the study highlights the role of cultural factors and the capabilities in promoting ambidexterity and supports the notion that cultural factors play an important role in shaping organizational behavior and performance. While the MBV highlights the role of market orientation and the design of the organization in shaping performance.

The study also makes a theoretical contribution by examining the impact of OA on performance. This contribution is significant because it highlights the potential benefits of OA and provides practical implications for organizations looking to improve their performance.

Finally, the use of covariance in the study provides a more robust and systematic way of examining the relationships between the variables and highlights the strengths and weaknesses of each variable in contributing to OA and performance. This approach allows for a more comprehensive understanding of the relationships between these variables and provides a more solid foundation for future research in the area.

Practical Contribution

The study makes four main contributions to practice.

Insights Into Relationships Between Themes and Their Impact on OAI

First, the study provides insights into the relationships between variables such as organizational culture, dynamic capabilities, market orientation, and organizational design, and their impact on OAI and performance. The study provides an improved understanding of the factors affecting OA implementation (OAI) and performance by exploring the relationships between various variables and their impact on OAI and performance.

Strength of the relationship between variables: the R2 statistic was used to measure the strength of the relationship between the endogenous constructs in the model, providing a measure of the model's ability to predict outcomes based on available data. The Independent Sample *t* test was used to assess differences in the performances of organizations by exploring the difference between high- and low-performing organizations based on their level of turnover. An SEM analysis allowed the researchers to determine the direction of causality between the variables and to examine the relative strength of each variable in contributing to OAI and its impact on organizational performance.

The study helped organizations identify the key drivers and barriers in implementing OAI, allowing them to make informed decisions on how to improve. By providing a more comprehensive understanding of the factors affecting OAI and performance, the study helps organizations to identify areas where they need to improve and make informed decisions on how to do so, leading to a more ambidextrous organization that is better equipped to handle the challenges of a rapidly changing business environment.

Diagnostic Tools With AI Algorithms to Improve Decision Making in Organizations

This study's investigation produced important results that have application to companies. It is possible to gain insightful knowledge and make useful contributions when comparing OA between high-performing and low-performing businesses.

First, the study found significant disparities between high-performing and low-performing businesses in a number of OA-related domains using *t* tests. The deployment of customer value-driven business strategies, regular customer visits, and resource sharing across business units are just a few examples of how high-performing firms have proven their superior skills. These findings emphasize how crucial these techniques are for obtaining high performance and offer managers useful advice. A diagnostic tool was also developed utilizing the AI/ML machine learning tool, based on the studies and the construction of the AI model. Managers can use this tool to compare their businesses to the dataset, which will allow them to gauge their level of OA and spot potential areas for improvement. This useful application gives managers a realistic tool for assessing the ambidexterity of their firm and for making wise choices that will improve performance.

This study provides a number of significant practical findings. First of all, it emphasizes the significance of particular procedures and actions that set high-performing firms apart from their less successful competitors. This suggests that in order to promote success and raise an organization's performance, managers must take these elements into account and prioritize them.

The creation of the diagnostic tool also gives enterprises a useful tool to assess their level of OA and benchmark themselves against a sizable dataset. Organizations can use this benchmarking capability to assess their ambidexterity implementation strengths and weaknesses and develop plans to improve performance.

Identifying Opportunity Areas for Improvement

The study also makes practical contributions by helping organizations identify areas for improvement. The study was able to analyze the relationships between different variables, such as organizational culture, dynamic capabilities, market orientation, and organizational design, and OAI. The results of the analysis provided organizations with valuable insights into the key drivers and barriers to implementing OAI and performance. This understanding can be used to identify areas where organizations need to improve in order to achieve a more ambidextrous organization that is better equipped to handle the challenges of a rapidly changing business environment. The study highlighted that for an organization's culture to be supportive of OAI, it must align with their organizational design. By identifying these areas, organizations makes targeted decisions to improve their OAI and overall performance. In this way, the study provides organizations with a roadmap for improvement, helping them to identify specific areas where they need to focus their efforts in order to achieve their desired outcomes. The study helps organizations identify areas where they need to improve, such as dynamic capabilities, organizational culture, and market orientation, to achieve a more ambidextrous organization that is better equipped to handle the challenges of a rapidly changing business environment.

Integrates Multiple Factor Relationships in Recommending Improvement Criteria

Lastly, this study takes a comprehensive approach to improving organizational performance, by considering multiple factors and their interrelationships, rather than focusing on just one or two variables. The study takes a holistic approach to improving organizational performance by considering multiple factors that impact OAI and performance. This holistic approach helps organizations to see the big picture and understand how different factors interact and impact OAI and performance. It also provides a more comprehensive understanding of the factors that drive OAI and performance, allowing organizations to make informed decisions about which factors to focus on in order to improve. By considering multiple factors and taking a holistic approach, the study helps organizations to improve their performance in a sustainable and effective manner. It also ensures that organizations do not overlook important factors that may impact OAI and performance, helping them to achieve a more balanced and well-rounded improvement in their operations. In this way, the study provides organizations with a comprehensive and holistic approach to improving their performance, helping them to achieve their desired outcomes and become more successful in the long term.

Implementation

Exploration

High-performing companies perform significantly differently from low-performing companies in some of their exploration strategies to OA implementation. The findings show that high-performing companies can explore resources from within and outside their domains. Their level of exploration allows them to survive and transform the pressure dynamics, take risks, make iterative changes in line with the current trends in the industry and apply structural changes to their management operation.

Exploitation

The result also shows that high-performing organizations ensure exploitation of all resources to the maximum and follow pre-set frameworks, emphasize on urgency linked to their short-term objectives, consider internal dynamics in their operations, and focus more on short-term objectives to help them align with their set objectives. This result is in alignment with the previous empirical assumption and this study's findings on the implementation of OA by organizations.

Coordinating Capability

High-performing organizations perform significantly different than their lower-performing counterparts based on the ability to explore the capabilities which enable organizations to co-ordinate in order to reconfigure existing operational capabilities into new ones that better match the environment. High-performing organizations are able to synchronize their output with the work of others in the industry, allocate appropriate resources, assign tasks that are commensurate with the knowledge and skills of employees and devote great time for the implementation of new products and ideas.

Integrating Capability

High-performing organizations perform significantly differently than their lower-performing counterparts based on the capacity to explore the capabilities which enable organizations to integrate in order to reconfigure existing operational capabilities into new ones that better match the environment. High-performing organizations integrate, contribute at group and individual levels, and interrelate with one another to create positive actions and interconnect the activities of members based on the overall goal of the organization. Therefore, their ability to integrate well within the industry will assist them to implement contextual ambidexterity.

Learning Capability

The results show that high-performing organizations perform significantly different from low-performing organizations in their ability to explore the capabilities which enable organizations to learn in order to reconfigure existing operational capabilities into new ones that better match the environment. Similarly, this finding aligns with the earlier assumptions that organizations should have effective routines to identify values and import new information and knowledge. Also, organizations should have adequate routines to assimilate new information and knowledge while utilizing the new knowledge and information in the development of new products and ideas.

Sensing Capability

This study identifies the potential of high-performing organizations to perform differently from low-performing organizations based on the ability to explore the capabilities which enable organizations to sense the environment in order to reconfigure existing operational capabilities into new ones that better match the environment. Sensing the environment to frequently scan and identify new business opportunities, periodically review likely changes in business and environmental patterns, review of product development and ideas are ways by which organizations perform better in implementing ambidexterity.

Group Diversity

This study identifies the potential of high-performing organizations to perform differently from low-performing organizations based on the actions within organizations that display organizational diversity. High-performing organizations perform differently due to their ability to respect everyone's different viewpoint in the organization irrespective of position and condition, and they also encourage all the employees to generate alternative solutions to problems for the organization. This position aligns with the earlier assumptions made for the study.

Shared Vision

The ability of organizations to make employees view themselves as partners in charting the direction of the organization, communicate the future direction of each business unit, include employees in the long-term planning, and give a strong sense of involvement differentiate a high-performing organization from a low-performing one. The resulting shared vision of an organization is important in achieving the objectives of the organization.

Customer Orientation

The results show that high-performing organizations place greater emphasis on objectives driven by customer satisfaction and the ability to monitor and assess the level of commitment of the organization in serving customers' needs, and the overall business strategy is anchored on increasing customer values.

Competitor Orientation

These findings show consistency with the empirical and literature findings that a high-performing organization's competitor orientation significantly differentiates them from low-performing organizations. High-performing salespersons have information about their competitors, respond rapidly to competition actions, regularly appraise and discuss the strengths and weaknesses of organizations, and focus on grabbing customers when there is opportunity for competitive advantage.

Inter-Functional Coordination

Again, in alignment with the empirical and normative findings of this study, the results showed that high-performing organizations perform better in their ability to share resources across the business units in the organization, to manage and understand how employees contribute to customer value, to regularly visit customers, and to apply business strategies driven by goals to achieve customer values.

Summary of the Chapter

This chapter presents the implications and discussion of the findings of the study on the relationship between OA and firm performance. The findings from both qualitative and quantitative approaches are presented and analyzed to provide insights into the implementation of OA in organizations and its impact on performance. The discussion focuses on the managerial decisions and actions that influence the implementation and embedding of OA, the key barriers and drivers to implementation, the variations in exploration and exploitation across industries, and the differences in managerial perspectives between low- and high-performing industries.

In addition, the chapter also presents the results from the development of a diagnostic tool to assess OA in organizations and recommends actions for improvement. The tool was developed using an AI/ML, to provide practical insights into the levels of OA in organizations. The discussion of the findings provides an in-depth analysis of the results and highlights the importance of considering OA in organizational decision-making.

The results of the study offer valuable insights into the OAI in organizations and its impact on performance. The implications and discussion of the findings suggest that managerial decisions and actions play a critical role in the implementation and embedding of OA. It is also highlighted that the implementation of OA is influenced by both internal and external factors, such as the organizational culture, resources, and the industry context.

Furthermore, the study's results suggest that the implementation of exploration and exploitation varies across industries and that managerial perspectives on OAI differ between low- and high-performing industries. These results emphasize the importance of considering the industry context when implementing OA and highlight the need for organizations to adopt a flexible approach to balancing exploration and exploitation. Overall, the implications and discussion of the findings provide practical insights into the implementation of OA in organizations and its impact on performance. The results of the study contribute to the body of knowledge on OA and offer valuable insights for organizations looking to improve their performance through the implementation of OA. The chapter concludes with a summary of the key implications and insights gained from the study and highlights the importance of further research in this area.

The study on the relationship between OA and firm performance provides valuable insights into the implementation of OA in organizations and its impact on performance. The findings from mixed approaches suggest that managerial decisions and actions are critical in the implementation and embedding of OA, and that the implementation of OA is influenced by both internal and external factors. The development of a diagnostic tool to assess OA in organizations offers practical insights into the levels of OA and recommends actions for improvement. The study's results also suggest that the implementation of exploration and exploitation varies across industries and that organizational performance is affected by the industry context. The implications and discussion of the findings provide practical insights into the implementation of OA in organizations and its impact on performance, contributing to the body of knowledge on OA and offering valuable insights for organizations looking to improve their performance.

The next chapter provides recommendations based on the findings of the study to assist organizations in implementing OA and improving their performance. These recommendations include actionable steps for managers to embed OA in their organizations.

Fostering an Effective Managerial Organizational Implementation of Ambidexterity

The study of OA and performance adopted qualitative and quantitative approaches which were explored through covariance analysis and a grounded theory research philosophy, which involves collecting and analyzing data to generate a theory that explains the phenomenon. The study aims to understand the relationship between OA and performance, and to provide insights into how organizations can convert ambidexterity into performance.

The study tested the relationship between OA and performance using covariance analysis and independent sample *t* test. The R2 statistic, obtained using the covariance analysis algorithm, showed that dynamic capability and organizational culture accounted for 54% of the variance in OA, and OA accounted for 54% of the variance in organizational performance. The *t* test revealed that low- and high-performing organizations had statistically different turnover rates. The study also used AI/ML to provide practical contributions to the field. Theoretically, the study contributes to the RBV and MBV theories by examining the impact of dynamic capability and organizational Culture on OA and performance. The study also focuses on the differences in the views of "high"- and "low"-performing companies on OA implementation and the barriers and drivers that can impact the implementation of OA in organizations. Additionally, the study also provides insights into the relationship between the implementation of exploration and exploitation across industries and the managerial perspectives on OA implementation across industries.

The study highlights the importance of understanding the specific needs of the industry and organization and finding the right balance between exploration and exploitation to achieve goals and remain competitive.

Conclusion

The integrated discussion and analysis of the study's findings on the relationship between OA and firm performance in Chapter 6 provide a comprehensive understanding of the complex factors influencing OA implementation and its impact on organizational performance. By synthesizing insights from both qualitative and quantitative approaches, the chapter offers a nuanced perspective on the critical role of managerial decisions, supportive organizational culture, clear communication, and resource allocation in the successful implementation and embedding of OA.

The development of a diagnostic tool using AI/ML represents a significant practical contribution, enabling organizations to assess their OA levels and identify areas for improvement. The study's theoretical contributions to the RBV and MBV further enrich the understanding of the relationships between dynamic capabilities, market orientation, organizational culture, and design in driving OA and performance.

The insights and recommendations provided in this chapter serve as a valuable guide for organizations seeking to achieve sustained success through the effective implementation of OA. However, the journey towards ambidexterity is an ongoing process that requires continuous adaptation and refinement. The subsequent chapter will delve into the conclusions drawn from the study and offer actionable recommendations for organizations looking to foster an effective managerial and organizational implementation of ambidexterity, taking into account the challenges and opportunities presented by an ever-changing business landscape.

7 Conclusion and Recommendations

Introduction

This chapter shares a concise summary and set of recommendations based on the insights and findings presented throughout the book on Organizational Ambidexterity (OA) and its relationship with firm performance. The chapter starts with a summary of all key areas across the book. It highlights the theoretical contributions of the book, integrating the Resource-Based View (RBV) and Market-Based View (MBV) perspectives to enrich the understanding of OA drivers and outcomes whilst emphasizing the practical implications of the study, introducing the Organizational Ambidexterity (OgAM) Tool, a diagnostic instrument developed through a rigorous 4-stage process involving data collection, AI/ML modeling with fuzzy logic, iterative feedback, and continuous improvement.

The OgAM Tool is an innovative and yet disruptive offering which would enable managers to self-diagnose their operations and identify tailored solutions for balancing efficiency and innovation. Additionally, the chapter shares a 12-point formula card and an Organizational Ambidexterity Multi-Phased Approach, offering actionable insights and a structured roadmap for successful OA implementation. In conclusion, the chapter emphasizing the importance of continuous learning, adaptation, and growth in the journey towards ambidexterity, highlighting the need for further research to explore the nuances and boundary conditions of OA in an ever-evolving business landscape.

Book Summary

This book has provided a comprehensive exploration of OA and its relationship with firm performance. By examining the concept of OA, its antecedents, consequences, and moderators, as well as the practical frameworks and strategies for its implementation, this text offers valuable insights for both academics and practitioners seeking to navigate the complexities of

DOI: 10.4324/9781003488224-7

balancing exploration and exploitation in today's dynamic business environment (O'Reilly & Tushman, 2013; Raisch & Birkinshaw, 2008).

The Concept of OA: as illustrated through the story of the Digital Dreamers, OA is a critical capability for organizations striving to simultaneously explore new opportunities and exploit existing competencies (March, 1991; Tushman & O'Reilly, 1996). The literature review revealed divergent perspectives on the core components of OA, with scholars debating the simultaneous or interdependent nature of exploration and exploitation (Benner & Tushman, 2003; Gupta et al., 2006). Despite these differing views, there is a consensus on the importance of OA for organizational success and the need for further research to unravel its complexities (Raisch & Birkinshaw, 2008).

Antecedents and Consequences of OA: the book examined the antecedents of OA, including structural, contextual, and leadership-based factors that influence an organization's ability to balance exploration and exploitation (Gibson & Birkinshaw, 2004; Raisch & Birkinshaw, 2008). The consequences of OA were also explored, highlighting its potential impact on innovation, adaptation, and overall performance (He & Wong, 2004; Jansen et al., 2009b). The Digital Dreamers' journey showcased the challenges and benefits of embracing OA, underlining the importance of understanding its drivers and outcomes.

Types of OA: the text delved into the various types of OA, including sequential, structural, and contextual ambidexterity (O'Reilly & Tushman, 2013; Tushman & O'Reilly, 1996). Each approach offers unique advantages and challenges, requiring organizations to carefully consider their specific needs and contexts when implementing OA strategies. The Digital Dreamers' evolution through these different approaches illustrated the importance of strategic fit and the need for continuous adaptation.

Organizational Culture and Ambidexterity

Organizational culture emerged as a critical factor in fostering ambidexterity, with the Competing Values Framework providing a useful lens for understanding the interplay between different cultural types (Cameron & Quinn, 2011; Schein, 2010). The story of Tech & Taste highlighted the importance of cultivating a culture that supports both stability and flexibility, enabling organizations to thrive in the face of change (Wang & Rafiq, 2014).

Organizational Agility and Dynamic Capabilities

The book explored the concepts of organizational agility and dynamic capabilities as key enablers of OA in turbulent markets (Teece et al., 1997,

2016). The narratives of Digital Dreamers and Katrina's Kitchen demonstrated how the convergence of these capabilities allows organizations to sense, seize, and reconfigure their resources to navigate market turbulence successfully (Eisenhardt & Martin, 2000; Helfat et al., 2007).

Organizational Design and Learning

The text examined the role of organizational design and learning in facilitating OA (Daft, 2018; Schein, 2010). By creating structures, processes, and systems that support both exploration and exploitation, organizations can create an environment conducive to ambidexterity (Tushman & O'Reilly, 1996). Continuous learning and knowledge sharing were also highlighted as essential for fostering innovation and adaptation (Argyris & Schön, 1978; March, 1991).

Implications for Theory and Practice

The findings of this book contribute to the theoretical understanding of OA by integrating the RBV and MBV perspectives (Barney, 1991; Porter, 1996). The empirical evidence provided supports the role of organizational culture, dynamic capabilities, market orientation, and organizational design as key drivers of OA and performance (Narver & Slater, 1990; Teece et al., 1997). These insights enrich the existing literature and provide a foundation for future research.

From a practical standpoint, the book offers valuable recommendations for organizations seeking to implement OA effectively. A significant contribution is the development of the Organizational Ambidexterity (OgAM) Tool, which enables managers to self-diagnose their operations and identify tailored solutions for balancing efficiency and innovation. The OgAM Tool was created through a rigorous four-stage process.

Stage 1

Data Collection: the foundation of the OgAM Tool was built on comprehensive data collection, including both qualitative and quantitative inputs. Qualitative data was gathered through interviews and surveys with industry leaders to understand their challenges and best practices in managing ambidexterity (Birkinshaw & Gupta, 2013).

Quantitative data was collected from a sample of 408 companies and *t* tests were conducted to identify the top 100 and bottom 100 performers based on organizational performance criteria, to determine the key factors enabling top performance, and to highlight the top factors responsible for at least a 30% variance between high and low performers (Lavie et al., 2010).

This analysis provided crucial insights into the attributes and practices distinguishing ambidextrous organizations.

Stage 2

AI/ML Model with Fuzzy Logic: the insights from Stage 1 were used to develop an AI/ML model leveraging fuzzy logic. The model tested attributes using data classifiers and assessed nearest neighbor correlation coefficients to confirm variance between high and low performers. This validated the effectiveness and efficiency of the dataset for machine learning (Simsek et al., 2009).

Fuzzy logic was deployed to convert crisp inputs into an inference engine and produce a defuzzified output. Fuzzy logic excels at modeling complex, non-linear systems by using linguistic variables and approximate reasoning (Zimmermann, 2010). For the OgAM Tool, fuzzy sets were defined for key attributes like "Structural Differentiation" and "Integration Mechanisms". Membership functions mapped crisp input values to degrees of membership between 0 and 1. Fuzzy rules then connected input combinations to ambidexterity levels. The inference engine aggregated rule outputs into a fuzzy output, which was defuzzified into a crisp ambidexterity score and recommendations.

Stage 3

Feedback from Trials: the OgAM Tool prototype was tested with three selected companies to gather feedback. Wireframes were presented to

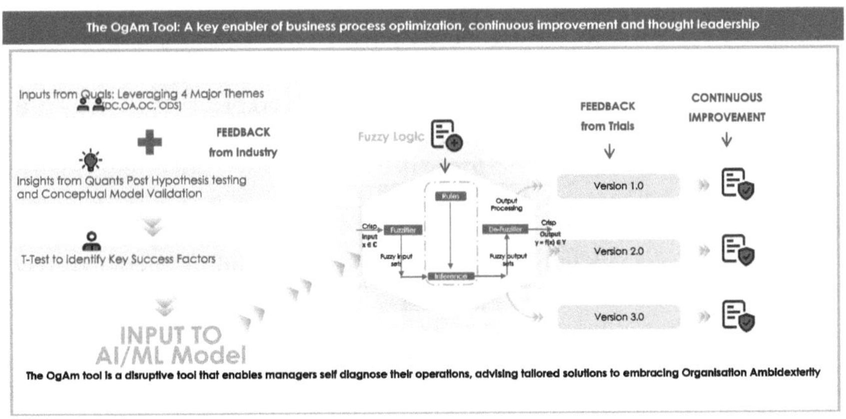

Figure 7.1 The OgAM Tool: Contribution to Practice

managers who input their organizational data and evaluated the tool's usability, clarity of outputs, and actionability of recommendations. Their feedback was incorporated to refine the user interface, fine-tune the fuzzy logic rules, and ensure the tool addressed real-world management needs (Raisch & Birkinshaw, 2008).

Stage 4

Continuous Improvement of MVP: the refined minimum viable product (MVP) was launched across ten companies for further validation and continuous improvement. Managers used the OgAM Tool to self-diagnose their ambidexterity and implemented the recommendations. Ongoing data collection monitored the tool's impact on key performance indicators. Feedback was regularly incorporated into new iterations to optimize the fuzzy logic model, expand the knowledge base, and enhance interpretability (Teece, 2007).

Contribution to Ambidexterity Practice

The finalized OgAM Tool contributes to business transformation by operationalizing a novel approach to OA (O'Reilly & Tushman, 2013). Its grounding in data analytics and fuzzy logic addresses limitations of prior subjective assessments. The tool's accessible, user-friendly format enables dynamic self-diagnosis and actionable recommendations.

By providing tailored guidance to balance efficiency and innovation, the OgAM Tool supports continuous improvement and long-term success. It serves as a key enabler of business process optimization, change management, and thought leadership to help organizations thrive in complex environments.

In conclusion, the four-stage development process of the OgAM Tool leveraged rigorous data analysis, cutting-edge AI techniques, and iterative feedback to create a validated, impactful solution. It represents an innovative application of fuzzy logic to the critical challenge of OA. As companies continue striving for sustainable performance, the OgAM Tool equips managers to effectively balance competing demands and adapt to an ever-changing business landscape.

This book has shed light on the complex and multifaceted nature of OA and its critical role in driving firm performance. By synthesizing theoretical perspectives, empirical evidence, and practical insights, it provides a comprehensive understanding of how organizations can effectively balance exploration and exploitation to thrive in today's dynamic business landscape (He & Wong, 2004; O'Reilly & Tushman, 2013).

As organizations continue to face the challenges of rapid technological change, globalization, and intense competition, the ability to simultaneously innovate and optimize becomes increasingly vital (Christensen, 1997; Eisenhardt & Martin, 2000). The insights and recommendations provided in this book serve as a valuable guide for leaders and managers seeking to cultivate ambidexterity within their organizations and harness its potential for sustainable growth and success.

While this text has made significant contributions to the understanding of OA, it also highlights the need for further research to explore its nuances and boundary conditions (Raisch & Birkinshaw, 2008). As the business environment continues to evolve, so too must our understanding of OA and its implications for organizational performance.

Ultimately, the journey towards ambidexterity is one of continuous learning, adaptation, and growth (March, 1991; Tushman & O'Reilly, 1996). By embracing the insights and strategies presented in this book, organizations can chart a course towards a more agile, innovative, and resilient future, equipped to navigate the challenges and opportunities that lie ahead.

Recommendations

Based on the findings and insights presented throughout this book, the following recommendations are offered to organizations seeking to effectively implement OA and enhance their performance. These have been distilled into a 12-point formula card:

Organizational Ambidexterity 12-point Formula card

1. **Develop a clear and compelling vision for OA**
   To successfully implement OA, organizations must articulate a clear and compelling vision that communicates the importance and benefits of ambidexterity (O'Reilly & Tushman, 2004a). This vision should be aligned with the organization's overall strategy and values, and should be effectively communicated to all stakeholders (Tushman & O'Reilly, 1996). Leaders should actively engage employees in the visioning process, fostering a sense of ownership and commitment to the OA journey (Raisch & Birkinshaw, 2008).
2. **Conduct a thorough assessment of organizational readiness for OA**
   Before embarking on the journey towards ambidexterity, organizations should conduct a comprehensive assessment of their current state (Roglinger et al., 2018a). This assessment should include an analysis of the organization's culture, structure, processes, and capabilities, as well as its external environment and competitive landscape (Gibson &

Birkinshaw, 2004; Raisch & Birkinshaw, 2008). The diagnostic tool developed using AI/ML, as discussed in Chapter 6, can serve as a valuable resource in this assessment process.

3. **Foster a culture of experimentation and learning**
As highlighted in the stories of Digital Dreamers and Tech & Taste, a culture that encourages experimentation, risk-taking, and continuous learning is essential for OA (March, 1991; Wang & Rafiq, 2014). Organizations should create an environment where employees feel empowered to explore new ideas, challenge assumptions, and learn from failures (Argyris & Schön, 1978). This can be achieved through initiatives such as innovation labs, hackathons, and cross-functional collaborations that promote creativity and knowledge sharing (O'Reilly & Tushman, 2004a).
4. **Establish clear governance mechanisms for OA**
To effectively balance exploration and exploitation, organizations must establish clear governance mechanisms that define roles, responsibilities, and decision-making processes (Tushman & O'Reilly III, 2013a). These mechanisms should be designed to facilitate coordination and collaboration across different units and levels of the organization, while also providing the necessary autonomy and flexibility for innovation (Gibson & Birkinshaw, 2004). Regular review and adjustment of these governance structures may be necessary as the organization evolves and learns (Raisch & Birkinshaw, 2008).
5. **Invest in dynamic capabilities development**
As discussed in Chapter 5, dynamic capabilities are critical for organizations operating in turbulent markets (Teece et al., 1997, 2016). To enhance their agility and adaptability, organizations should invest in the development of key dynamic capabilities such as sensing, seizing, and reconfiguring (Eisenhardt & Martin, 2000; Helfat et al., 2007). This can be achieved through targeted training programs, strategic partnerships, and the cultivation of a learning-oriented mindset throughout the organization (Teece, 2007).
6. **Align organizational design with OA goals**
The organizational design should be aligned with the goals and strategies of OA (Tushman & O'Reilly, 1996). This may involve the creation of dedicated exploration and exploitation units, as well as the establishment of cross-functional teams and networks that facilitate knowledge flow and collaboration (Gibson & Birkinshaw, 2004). Organizations should also consider the physical design of their workspaces, ensuring that they promote interaction, creativity, and flexibility (Schein, 2010).
7. **Leverage technology to support OA**
Technology can play a crucial role in enabling OA by facilitating communication, collaboration, and data-driven decision-making

(Sambamurthy et al., 2003). Organizations should invest in digital platforms and tools that support knowledge management, project management, and performance tracking (Jansen et al., 2009b). Advanced technologies such as artificial intelligence and machine learning can also be leveraged to identify new opportunities, optimize processes, and enhance organizational learning (Roglinger et al., 2018b).

8. **Develop ambidextrous leadership capabilities**
Leadership plays a critical role in driving OA, as demonstrated in the stories of Patricia and Alex (O'Reilly & Tushman, 2004a). Organizations should invest in the development of ambidextrous leadership capabilities, equipping leaders with the skills and mindsets needed to navigate the tensions and paradoxes of exploration and exploitation (Smith & Tushman, 2005a). This can be achieved through leadership development programs, mentoring, and coaching initiatives that focus on strategic agility, emotional intelligence, and adaptive decision-making (Tushman & O'Reilly III, 2013b).
9. **Measure and monitor OA progress**
To ensure the effectiveness of OA implementation, organizations must establish clear metrics and monitoring mechanisms (Jansen et al., 2009b). These should include both quantitative and qualitative measures that capture the progress and impact of exploration and exploitation activities (He & Wong, 2004). Regular reporting and review of these metrics can help identify areas for improvement and inform ongoing adjustments to the OA strategy (O'Reilly & Tushman, 2004b).
10. **Celebrate and communicate OA successes**
To maintain momentum and engagement in the OA journey, organizations should actively celebrate and communicate their successes (Tushman & O'Reilly, 1996). This can include sharing stories of innovative projects, recognizing individuals and teams who exemplify ambidextrous behaviors, and communicating the business impact of OA initiatives (Raisch & Birkinshaw, 2008). By showcasing the tangible benefits of ambidexterity, organizations can reinforce the importance of OA and inspire ongoing commitment to the journey (Gibson & Birkinshaw, 2004).
11. **Foster external partnerships and ecosystems**
Organizations should actively seek out external partnerships and engage in ecosystem development to enhance their OA capabilities (Chesbrough, 2003). This can include collaborations with startups, universities, and other organizations that bring diverse perspectives and capabilities to the table (Raisch & Birkinshaw, 2008). By leveraging external networks and resources, organizations can accelerate their learning, tap into new sources of innovation, and build resilience in the face of market disruptions (Teece, 2007).

12. **Continuously adapt and refine the OA approach**
    Implementing OA is not a one-time event, but rather an ongoing journey of learning and adaptation (March, 1991; Tushman & O'Reilly, 1996). Organizations must continually assess and refine their OA approach based on internal and external feedback, changing market conditions, and emerging best practices (O'Reilly & Tushman, 2004a). This requires a culture of continuous improvement, a willingness to experiment and pivot, and a commitment to long-term success (Raisch & Birkinshaw, 2008).

Organizational Ambidexterity Multi-Phased Formula Card

The earlier stated organizational ambidexterity formula card will be streamlined into three phases of execution which organizations can deploy to drive simplicity in execution:

Phase 1: Strategic Foundations

1. Develop a clear and compelling vision for OA – **Ideate**
2. Conduct a thorough assessment of organizational readiness for OA – **Analysis**
3. Establish clear governance mechanisms for OA – **Governance**
4. Align organizational design with OA goals – **Alignment**

Phase 2: Culture and Capabilities

5. Foster a culture of experimentation and learning – **Culture**
6. Invest in dynamic capabilities development – **Capabilities**
7. Develop ambidextrous leadership capabilities – **Leadership**
8. Foster external partnerships and ecosystems – **Partnerships**

Phase 3: Implementation and Refinement

9. Leverage Technology to support OA – **Technology**
10. Measure and monitor OA progress – **Control**
11. Celebrate and communicate OA successes – **Recognition**
12. Continuously adapt and refine the OA approach – **Refinement**

Phase 1: Strategic Foundations

The first group focuses on laying the strategic groundwork for successful OA implementation. By conducting a thorough assessment, developing a clear vision, establishing governance mechanisms, and aligning organizational

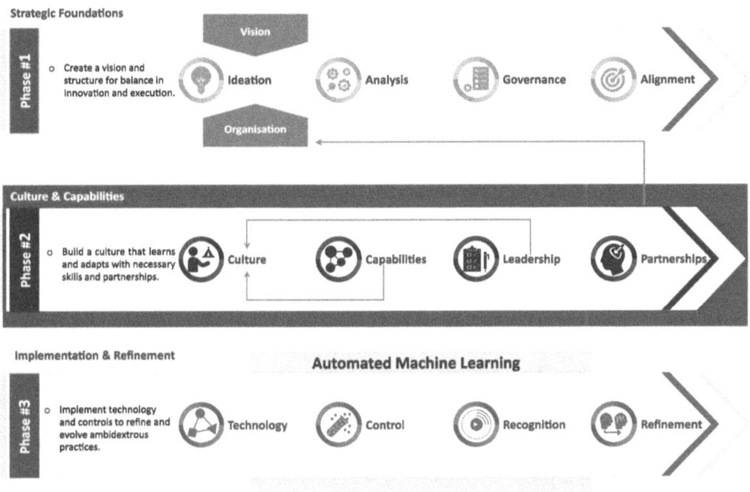

Figure 7.2 Organizational Ambidexterity Multi-Phased Formula Card

design, organizations can create a solid foundation for their ambidexterity journey.

Phase 2: Culture and Capabilities

The second group emphasizes the importance of cultivating an organizational culture and capabilities that support OA. Fostering a culture of experimentation and learning, investing in dynamic capabilities, developing ambidextrous leadership, and leveraging external partnerships are key elements in building an environment conducive to ambidexterity.

Phase 3: Implementation and Refinement

The third group addresses the practical aspects of implementing and refining the OA approach. Leveraging technology, measuring progress, celebrating successes, and continuously adapting are essential for ensuring the effectiveness and sustainability of OA initiatives.

By categorizing the recommendations into these three groups, organizations can take a structured and comprehensive approach to implementing OA. Each group represents a critical pillar in the OA journey, and by addressing the elements within each group, organizations can increase their chances of success in balancing exploration and exploitation for superior performance.

Conclusion

This book has provided a comprehensive exploration of OA and its relationship with firm performance. By examining the concept of OA, its antecedents, consequences, and moderators, as well as the practical frameworks and strategies for its implementation, this text offers valuable insights for both academics and practitioners seeking to navigate the complexities of balancing exploration and exploitation in today's dynamic business environment (O'Reilly & Tushman, 2013; Raisch & Birkinshaw, 2008).

The findings of this book contribute to the theoretical understanding of OA by integrating the RBV and MBV perspectives (Barney, 1991; Porter, 1996). The empirical evidence provided supports the role of organizational culture, dynamic capabilities, market orientation, and organizational design as key drivers of OA and performance (Narver & Slater, 1990; Teece et al., 1997). These insights enrich the existing literature and provide a foundation for future research.

From a practical standpoint, the book offers valuable recommendations for organizations seeking to implement OA effectively. The development of the Organizational Ambidexterity (OgAM) Tool, which enables managers to self-diagnose their operations and identify tailored solutions for balancing efficiency and innovation, represents a significant contribution. The OgAM Tool, created through a rigorous five-stage process involving data collection, AI/ML modeling with fuzzy logic, feedback from trials, continuous improvement of the MVP, and contribution to ambidexterity practice, showcases an innovative application of fuzzy logic to the critical challenge of OA (O'Reilly & Tushman, 2013; Zimmermann, 2010).

Moreover, the book presents a comprehensive 12-point formula card and an Organizational Ambidexterity Multi-Phased Approach, which provide actionable insights and a roadmap for managers navigating the challenges of OA implementation (O'Reilly & Tushman, 2004; Tushman & O'Reilly III, 2013b). The Multi-Phased Approach streamlines the 12-point formula card into three phases of execution: Strategic Foundations, Culture and Capabilities, and Implementation and Refinement. This structured approach enables organizations to drive simplicity in execution and increases their chances of success in balancing exploration and exploitation for superior performance.

As organizations continue to face the challenges of rapid technological change, globalization, and intense competition, the ability to simultaneously innovate and optimize becomes increasingly vital (Christensen, 1997; Eisenhardt & Martin, 2000). The insights, recommendations, and practical tools provided in this book serve as valuable guides for leaders and managers seeking to cultivate ambidexterity within their organizations and harness its potential for sustainable growth and success.

While this text has made significant contributions to the understanding of OA, it also highlights the need for further research to explore its nuances and boundary conditions (Raisch & Birkinshaw, 2008). As the business environment continues to evolve, so too must our understanding of OA and its implications for organizational performance.

Ultimately, the journey towards ambidexterity is one of continuous learning, adaptation, and growth (March, 1991; Tushman & O'Reilly, 1996). By embracing the insights, strategies, and tools presented in this book, including the OgAM Tool, the 12-point formula card, and the Organizational Ambidexterity Multi-Phased Approach, organizations can chart a course towards a more agile, innovative, and resilient future, equipped to navigate the challenges and opportunities that lie ahead.

Bibliography

Aftab, J., Veneziani, M., Sarwar, H., & Ishaq, M. I. (2022). OA, firm performance, and sustainable development: Mediating role of entrepreneurial orientation in Pakistani SMEs. *Journal of Cleaner Production*, *367*, 132956.

Agarwal, P. (2018). How to create a positive workplace culture. *Forbes*.

Agostini, L., Nosella, A., & Filippini, R. (2016). Towards an integrated view of the ambidextrous organization: A second-order factor model. *Creativity and Innovation Management*, *25*(1), 129–141.

Alder, P., Goldoftas, B., & Levine, D. (1999). Flexibility versus efficiency? A case study of model changeovers in the Toyota production system. *Organization Science*, *10*(1), 43–68.

Alder, P., & Heckscher, C. (2015). Contextual ambidexterity and the value-rational organizational form.

Alpkan, L., Şanal, M., & Ayden, Y. (2012). Market orientation, ambidexterity and performance outcomes. *Procedia – Social and Behavioral Sciences*, *41*, 461–468.

Amit, R., & Schoemaker, P. J. H. (1993). Strategic assets and organizational rent. *Strategic Management Journal*, *14*(1), 33–46.

Anderson, J. C., Day, G. S., & Rangan, V. K. (2016). The role of strategic alliances in the evolution of the healthcare industry. *Strategic Management Journal*, *37*(10), 2044–2061.

Anderson, R. C., & Anderson, D. (2016). OA: Past, present, and future. *Academy of Management Perspectives*, *30*(2), 167–180.

Andriopoulos, C., & Lewis, M. W. (2009). Exploitation-exploration tensions and organizational ambidexterity: Managing paradoxes of innovation. *Organization Science*, *20*(4), 696–717.

Antwi, S., & Kasim, H. (2015). Qualitative and quantitative research paradigms in business research: A philosophical reflection. *European Journal of Business and Management*, *7*, 217–225.

Argote, L., & Greve, H. R. (2007). In search of the missing link: Understanding how contextual factors shape mindsets. *Academy of Management Review*, *32*(2), 404–424.

Argyris, C., & Schön, D. A. (1978). *Organizational learning: A theory of action perspective*. Addison-Wesley.

Baker, W. E., & Sinkula, M. (2005). Market orientation and the new product paradox. *Journal of Product Innovation Management*, 22(6), 483–502.

Bandura, A. (1997). *Self-efficacy: The exercise of control*. Freeman.

Barcelos, E. J. B. V., Amatucci, M., Borini, F. M., & Raziq, M. M. (2022). Renewing a subsidiary's innovative capabilities through flexible design, contextual

ambidexterity, and external embeddedness. *Revista Brasileira de Gestão de Negócios, 24*, 556–573.
Barney, J. (1991). Firm resources and sustained competitive advantages. *Journal of Management, 17*(1), 99–120.
Barney, J. (1995). Looking inside for competitive advantage. *The Academy of Management Executive, 9*(4), 49–61.
Baskarad, S., & Koronious, A. (2018). The 5S organizational agility framework: A dynamic capabilities perspective. *International Journal of Organizational Analysis, 26*(2).
Batra, I., & Dhir, S. (2022). OA from the emerging market perspective: A review and research agenda. *Thunderbird International Business Review, 64*(5), 559–573.
Baum, J. (Ed.) (2017). *Companion to organizations* (pp. 281–303). Blackwell.
Benner, M. J., & Tushman, M. L. (2003). Exploitation, exploration, and process management: The productivity dilemma revisited. *Academy of Management Review, 28*(2), 238–256.
Berthon, P., Hulbert, J. M., & Pitt, L. F. (1999). To serve or create? Strategic orientations toward customers and innovation. *California Management Review, 42*(1), 37–58.
Birkinshaw, J., & Gibson, C. (2004). Building ambidexterity into an organization. *Sloan Management Review, 45*(4), 47–55.
Birkinshaw, J., & Gupta, K. (2013). Clarifying the distinctive contribution of ambidexterity to the field of organization studies. *Academy of Management Perspectives, 27*(4), 287–298.
Blanche, M. T., Durrheim, K., & Painter, D. (2016). *Research in practice: Applied methods for the social sciences.* UTC Press.
Boje, D. (2001). What is critical post-modern theory.
Botha, J., van der Westhuizen, D., & De Swardt, E. (2005). Towards appropriate methodologies to research interactive learning: Using a design experiment to assess a learning programme for complex thinking development. *International Journal of Education and Development using ICT, 1*(2). http://ijedict.dec.uwi.edu/viewarticle.php?id=43
Boumgarden, P., Nickerson, J., & Zenger, T. R. (2012). Sailing into the wind: Exploring the relationships among ambidexterity, vacillation, and organizational performance. *Strategic Management Journal, 33*(6), 587–610. https://doi.org/10.1002/smj.1972
Braun, V., & Clarke, V. (2006). Using thematic analysis in psychology. *Qualitative Research in Psychology, 3*(2), 77–101.
Brown, S. L., & Eisenhardt, K. M. (1997). The art of continuous change: Linking complexity theory and time-paced evolution in relentlessly shifting organizations. *Administrative Science Quarterly, 42*(1), 1–34.
Bucherer, E., Eisert, U., & Gassmann, O. (2012). Towards systematic experimentation in business model innovation. In M. J. Fischer & P. T. C. Sanders (Eds.), *Proceedings of the 2012 European conference on innovation and entrepreneurship* (pp. 73–81). Academic Conferences International Limited.
Cameron, K. S., & Quinn, R. E. (1999). *Diagnosing and changing organizational culture: Based on the competing values framework.* Addison-Wesley.
Cameron, K. S., & Quinn, R. E. (2006). *Diagnosing and changing organizational culture based on the competing values framework.* John Wiley & Sons.
Cameron, K. S., & Quinn, R. E. (2011). *Diagnosing and changing organizational culture: Based on the competing values framework* (3rd ed.). Jossey-Bass.
Cao, Q., Gedajlovic, E., & Zhang, H. (2009). Unpacking OA: Dimensions, contingencies, and synergistic effects. *Organization Science, 20*, 781–796.

Chen, E. L., & Katila, R. (2008). Rival interpretations of balancing exploration and exploitation: Simultaneous or sequential? In S. Shane (Ed.), *Handbook of technology and innovation management* (pp. 197–214). Wiley.

Chen, M.-J., & Miller, D. (2011). Competitive attack, response, and the structure of rivalry: A dynamic analysis. *Academy of Management Journal, 54*(6), 1205–1225.

Chen, Y., Huang, X., & Yan, R. (2019). Artificial intelligence in education: Past, present, and future. *Journal of Educational Technology Development and Exchange, 2*(1), 1–22.

Chesbrough, H. (2003). *Open innovation: The new imperative for creating and profiting from technology*. Harvard Business Review Press.

Chesbrough, H. (2018). *Open innovation: Researching a new paradigm*. Oxford University Press.

Chesbrough, H., & Bogers, M. (2014). Explicating open innovation: Clarifying an emerging paradigm for understanding innovation. In *New Frontiers in open innovation* (pp. 3–28). Oxford University Press.

Chien, S. W., & Tsai, C. Y. (2018). How leadership style and strategy type affect organizational culture and effectiveness in higher education. *Studies in Higher Education, 43*(9), 1554–1572.

Choi, J., & Lee, H. (2009). The role of information technology in improving organizational performance. *Journal of Strategic Information Systems, 18*(3), 179–190.

Chollet, F. (2018). *Deep learning with Python*. Manning Publications Co.

Chou, C., Yang, K., & Chiu, Y.-J. (2014). Managing sequential ambidexterity: Roles of temporal switching capability and contingent factors. *Academy of Management Proceedings, 2014*, 13537–13537. https://doi.org/10.5465/AMBPP.2014.13537abstract

Christensen, C. M. (1997). *The innovator's dilemma: When new technologies cause great firms to fail*. Harvard Business Review Press.

Christensen, C. M., & Bower, J. L. (1996). Customer power, strategic investment, and the failure of leading firms. *Strategic Management Journal, 17*(3), 197–218.

Christensen, C. M., Johnson, M. W., & Rigby, D. K. (2002). *The innovator's solution: Creating and sustaining successful growth*. Harvard Business Review Press.

Čiutienė, R., & Thattakath, E. (2015). Influence of dynamic capabilities in creating disruptive innovation. *Economics and Business*, 26. https://doi.org/10.7250/eb.2014.015

Coates, J., & McDermott, M. (2002). The impact of human resource management on organizational performance: An empirical analysis. *International Journal of Human Resource Management, 13*(3), 350–367.

Coffie, I. S., & Hinson, R. E. (2022). Market orientation in the public sector: The perspective from an emerging economy. In *New public management in Africa* (pp. 17–45). Palgrave Macmillan.

Cohen, L., Manion, L., & Morrison, K. (2007). *Research methods in education* (6th ed.). Routledge/Taylor & Francis Group.

Collis, D. J., & Montgomery, C. A. (1995). *Competing on resources: Strategy in the 1990s*. Harvard Business School Press.

Collis, D. J., & Montgomery, C. A. (2005). *Corporate strategy: Resources and the scope of the firm*. McGraw-Hill Education.

Collis, D. J., & Montgomery, C. A. (2008). Competing on resources: Strategy in the 1990s. *Harvard Business Review, 73*(4), 118–128.

Colotta, M., Becker, A., Wagner, M., & van den Berg, H. (2003).

Coltman, T., & Devinney, M. (2013). Modeling the operational capabilities for customized and commoditized services. *Journal of Operations Management, 31*, 555–566.

Concepta, T. (2012). *The role of organizational capabilities in the realization of organizational objectives at HELB in Kenya* [Master's thesis, University of Nairobi].

Covin, J. G., & Slevin, D. P. (1991). Strategic management of small firms in hostile and benign environments. *Strategic Management Journal*, *12*(1), 75–87.

Creswell, J. (2013). *Qualitative inquiry and research design: Choosing among five approaches*. SAGE Publications.

Creswell, J. W. (2014). *Research design: Qualitative, quantitative, and mixed methods approaches*. Sage Publications.

Creswell, J. W. (2018). *Mixed methods research: Design and procedures* (4th ed.). Sage.

Creswell, J. W., & Creswell, J. D. (2018). *Research design: Qualitative, quantitative, and mixed methods approaches*. Sage Publications.

Curado, C. (2014a). Managing knowledge for competitive advantage. *Knowledge Management Research & Practice*, *12*(3), 248–259.

Curado, C. (2014b). The impact of knowledge management on organizational performance. *Journal of Knowledge Management*, *18*(2), 156–175.

Daft, R. L. (2018). *Organization theory and design* (13th ed.). Cengage Learning.

Daveni, R., & Thomas, L. (2004). The rise of hyper competition in the US manufacturing sector, 1950 to 2002.

D'Aveni, R. A. (1994). *Hypercompetition: Managing the dynamics of strategic maneuvering*. Free Press.

Day, G. S. (1994). The capabilities of market-driven organizations. *Journal of Marketing*, *58*(4), 37–52.

Denning, S. (2011). How do you change an organizational culture. *Forbes*.

Denzin, N. K., & Lincoln, Y. S. (2011). *The SAGE handbook of qualitative research* (4th ed.). Sage.

Deshpande, R., Farley, J. U., & Webster, F. J. (1993). Corporate culture, customer orientation, and innovativeness. *Journal of Marketing*, *57*(1), 23.

Dickson, P. R. (1996). The static and dynamic mechanics of competitive theory. *Journal of Marketing*, 60(October), 102–106.

Dierickx, I., & Cool, K. (1989). Asset stock accumulation and sustainability of competitive advantage. *Management Science*, *35*(12), 1504–1511.

Doshi, N., & McGregor, L. (2015). How company culture shapes employee motivation. *Harvard Business Review*.

Dosi, G., Nelson, R. R., & Winter, S. G. (2000). *The nature and dynamics of organizational capabilities*. Oxford University Press.

Dove, R. (1999). *Knowledge management, decision making, and competitiveness*. Butterworth-Heinemann.

Dove, R. (2002). *The discipline of knowledge management*. Butterworth-Heinemann.

Doz, Y., & Kosonen, M. (2008). *Fast strategy: How strategic agility will help you stay ahead of the game*. Pearson/Longman, p. 65.

Doz, Y., & Kosonen, M. (2010). Embedding strategic agility: A leadership agenda for accelerating business model renewal. *Long Range Planning*, *43*(2–3), 370–382.

Dranev, Y., Izosimova, A., & Meissner, D. (2020). OA and performance: Assessment approaches and empirical evidence. *Journal of the Knowledge Economy*, *11*(2), 676–691.

Duncan, R. B. (1976). The ambidextrous organization: Designing dual structures for innovation. *The Management of Organization*, *1*, 167–188.

Eisenhardt, K., Furr, N., & Bingham, C. (2010). Microfoundations of performance: Balancing efficiency and flexibility in dynamic environments. *Organization Science*, *21*(6), 1263–1273.

Eisenhardt, K., & Martin, J. (2000). Dynamic capabilities: What are they? *Strategic Management Journal*, *21*, 1105–1121.

Ethiraj, S. K., Kale, P., Krishnan, M. S., & Singh, J. V. (2005). Where do capabilities come from and how do they matter? A study in the software services industry. *Strategic Management Journal*, *26*(1), 25–45.

Fang, E., Palmatier, R. W., & Steenkamp, J.-B. E. M. (2010). Inside the black box: The role of organizational culture in explaining the relationship between corporate social responsibility and firm performance. *Journal of Marketing*, *74*(2), 1–18.

Felin, T., & Powell, T. C. (2016). Designing organizations for dynamic capabilities. *California Management Review*, *58*(4), 78–96.

Figueiredo, P. N. (2003). Organizational culture and performance: A review and synthesis. *Journal of Business Research*, *56*(6), 462–470.

Floyd, S., & Lane, P. (2000). Strategizing throughout the organization: Managing role conflict in strategic renewal. *Academy of Management Review*, *25*, 154–177.

Flynn, B. B., Jayaram, J., & Ketokivi, M. (1995). Empirical research methods in operations management. *Journal of Operations Management*, *13*(2), 155–172.

Fujimoto, Y., & Kaneko, K. (2019). Emergence of exploitation as symmetry breaking in iterated prisoner's dilemma. *Physical Review Research*, *1*, 033077.

Gai, K., Huang, X., & Liu, Y. (2018). Artificial intelligence in big data era. *Journal of Big Data*, *5*(1), 1–12.

Garaus, M., Hutter, K., & Hoyer, W. D. (2012). The influence of brand reputation and consumer trust on brand loyalty: A study of the mobile phone industry. *Journal of Brand Management*, *19*(4), 314–332.

García-Hurtado, D., Devece, C., Zegarra-Saldaña, P. E., & Crisanto-Pantoja, M. (2022). Ambidexterity in entrepreneurial universities and performance measurement systems. A literature review. *International Entrepreneurship and Management Journal*, 1–22.

Gastaldi, L., Lessanibahri, S., Tedaldi, G., & Miragliotta, G. (2022). Companies' adoption of smart technologies to achieve structural ambidexterity: An analysis with SEM. *Technological Forecasting and Social Change*, *174*, 121187.

Gåsvaer, D., Stålberg, L., Fundin, A., Jackson, M., & Johansson, P. (2015). Exploration and exploitations within operations. International Journal of Economics and Management Engineering, *9*(8), 2380–2385.

Gephart, R. (1999). Paradigms and research methods. *Academy of Management*, *4*. http://division.aomonline.org/rm/1999_RMD_Forum_Paradigms_and_Research_Methods.htm

Ghonim, M. A., Zakaria Elsawy, W., Elsotouhy, M., & Khashan, M. A. (2022). Market orientation and new product development performance in Egyptian food industry: The mediating role of marketing technical integration. *Journal of Food Products Marketing*, *28*, 193–209.

Gibson, C. B., & Birkinshaw, J. (2004). The antecedents, consequences, and mediating role of OA. *Academy of Management Journal*, *47*(2), 209–226.

Giddens, A. (1984). *The constitution of society: Outline of the theory of structuration*. University of California Press.

Golder, P. N., & Tellis, G. J. (2004). Growing, growing, gone: Cascades, diffusion, and turning points in the product life cycle. *Marketing Science*, *23*(2), 207–218.

Goldman, S. P., & Nagel, R. N. (1993). *Management, technology, and innovation: A business process perspective*. John Wiley & Sons.

Goossen, M. C., Bazzazian, N., & Phelps, C. (2012). Consistently capricious: The performance effects of simultaneous and sequential ambidexterity.

Academy of Management Proceedings, 2012(1). https://doi.org/10.5465/AMBPP.2012.16311abstract

Grant, R. M. (1991). The resource-based theory of competitive advantage: Implications for strategy formulation. *California Management Review, 33*(3), 114–135.

Greer, C. R., Caruso, H. M., & Jehn, K. A. (2017). The effects of group composition and structure on group outcomes: A meta-analysis. *Journal of Management, 43*(2), 413–445.

Guest, G., MacQueen, K. M., & Namey, E. E. (2012). *Applied thematic analysis*. Sage.

Gulati, R., Dialdin, D. A., & Wang, L. (2002). Organizational networks. In *The Blackwell Companion to Organizations* (pp. 281–303). Wiley.

Gupta, A., Smith, K., & Shalley, C. (2006). The interplay between exploration and exploitation. *Academy of Management Journal, 49*(4), 693–706.

Gupta, A. K., & Govindarajan, V. (2000). Knowledge management's social dimension: Lessons from Nucor Steel. *Sloan Management Review, 42*(1), 71–80.

Gupta, A. K., & Krishnan, R. (2009). Dynamic capabilities and strategic management. *Journal of Business Research, 62*(1), 1–11.

Hair, J. F., Black, W. C., Babin, B. J., Anderson, R. E., & Tatham, R. L. (2006). *Multivariate data analysis* (6th ed.). Pearson Prentice Hall.

Halonen, N., & Majuri, M. (2019). Capability building through dynamic capabilities and organizational learning.

Hambrick, D. C., & Cannella, A. A. (1989). Strategy implementation as substance and as reflection of top management. In J. J. Shendel & C. L. Cooper (Eds.), *The strategic management handbook* (pp. 131–145). Pergamon Press.

Hamed, S., Ali, A., & Ahmed, S. (2018). Innovation and organizational performance: A review. *International Journal of Management Reviews, 20*(3), 295–316.

Hamel, G., & Prahalad, C. K. (1996). Competing for the future. *Harvard Business Review*.

Hammersley, M. (2013). *What is qualitative research?* Bloomsbury Academic, 125pp.

Hansen, E., Samuel, W., & Schaltegger, S. (2019). Structural ambidexterity, transition processes, and integration tradeoffs: A longitudinal study of failed exploration. *R&D Management, 49*, 484–508.

Harreld, J. B., O'Reilly, C. A., III, & Tushman, M. L. (2007). Dynamic capabilities at IBM: Driving strategy into action. *California Management Review, 49*(4), 21–43.

He, Z., & Wong, C. Y. (2020). Exploring the relationship between strategic ambidexterity and firm performance: The role of dynamic capabilities. *Journal of Business Research, 110*, 303–312.

Helfat, C., Finkelstein, S., Mitchell, W., Peteraf, M. A., Singh, H., Teece, D., & Winter, S. (2007). Dynamic capabilities and organizational process.

Helfat, C., & Peteraf, M. (2009). Understanding dynamic capabilities: Progress along a developmental path. *Strategic Organization, 7*(1), 91–102.

Helfat, C. E., Finkelstein, S., Mitchell, W., Peteraf, M. A., Singh, H., Teece, D. J., & Winter, S. G. (2009). *Dynamic capabilities: Understanding strategic change in organizations*. Blackwell Publishing.

Helfat, C. M., & Martin, J. A. (2015). Dynamic capabilities: An introduction. In C. M. Helfat & J. A. Martin (Eds.), *The Oxford handbook of dynamic capabilities* (pp. 1–20). Oxford University Press.

Helfat, C. M., & Peteraf, M. A. (2003). The dynamic resource-based view: Capability lifecycles. *Strategic Management Journal, 24*(10), 997–1010.

Helfat, C. M., & Peteraf, M. A. (2015). Managerial cognitive capabilities and the ambidexterity-performance relationship. *Strategic Management Journal, 36*(2), 121–136.

Henderson, R., & Cockburn, I. (1996). Scale, scope, and spillovers: The determinants of research productivity in drug discovery. *The RAND Journal of Economics, 27*(1), 32–59.

Hernández-Linares, R., Kellermanns, F. W., & López-Fernández, M. C. (2021). Dynamic capabilities and SME performance: The moderating effect of market orientation. *Journal of Small Business Management, 59*(1), 162–195.

He, Z. L., & Wong, P. K. (2004). Exploration vs. exploitation: An empirical test of the ambidexterity hypo. *Organization Science, 15*(4), 481–494.

Hill, C. W. L., & Jones, T. M. (2012). *Strategic management: An integrated approach* (10th ed.). Cengage Learning.

Hock, M., Shulz, E., & Claus, T. (2015). The impact of organizational culture on a firm's capability to innovate the business model. *R&D Management, 46*(3).

Hofstede, G. (1997). *Culture and organization: Software of the mind*. McGraw-Hill.

Holland, J. L. (1992) *Making vocational choices: A theory of vocational personalities and work environments* (3rd ed.). Psychological Assessment Resources.

Howard, A. (2016). What are the six critical organizational capabilities? *Psychosynthesis Coaching.*

Hrebiniak, L. G. (2006). Obstacles to effective strategy implementation. *Organizational Dynamics, 35*(1), 12–31.

Hu, Y., & Wang, D. (2018). OA and performance: A meta-analytic review and contingency perspective. *Journal of Business Research, 88*, 384–397.

Ireland, R. D., Hitt, M. A., & Sirmon, D. G. (2003). A model of strategic entrepreneurship: The construct and its dimensions. *Journal of Management, 29*(6), 963–989.

Jansen, J. (2005). Ambidextrous organizations: A multiple-level study of absorptive capacity, exploratory and exploitative innovation and performance.

Jansen, J., Vera, D., & Crossan, M. (2009a). Strategic leadership for exploration and exploitation: The moderating role of environmental dynamism. *The Leadership Quarterly, 20*(1), 5–18.

Jansen, J. J. P., Van Den Bosch, F. A. J., & Volberda, H. W. (2009b). Innovation and organizational performance: The role of ambidexterity. *Management Science, 55*(5), 787–802.

Javalgi, R. R., & White, D. S. (2011). Business-to-business exporting: Empirical evidence from U.S. firms. *Journal of Business Research, 64*(6), 701–708.

Jaworski, B. J., & Kohli, A. K. (1993). Market orientation: Antecedents and consequences. *Journal of Marketing.*

Jerry, W. (2007). *Foundations of qualitative research: Interpretive and critical approaches.* Thousand Oaks, CA: Sage Publications Inc., 367 pages.

Johansson, J., Jacobsson, S., & Rönnbäck, Å. (2017). Exploring resource endowment and open innovation: A study of Swedish manufacturing firms. *Industry and Innovation, 24*(2), 159–176.

Johnson, R. B., & Onwuegbuzie, A. J. (2004). Mixed methods research: A research paradigm whose time has come. *Educational Researcher, 33*(7), 14–26.

Kaplan, R. S., & Norton, D. P. (1992). The balanced scorecard—measures that drive performance. *Harvard Business Review, 70*(1), 71–79.

Kapur, R. (2018). Research methodology: Methods and strategies.

Karami, M., O'Reilly, M. M., & Anderson, L. (2020). Dynamic capabilities, competitive advantage, and firm performance: A multi-country study. *International Journal of Management Reviews, 22*(1), 112–130.

Katila, R., & Ahuja, G. (2002). Something old, something new: A longitudinal study of innovation and performance in the software industry. *Management Science*, *48*(8), 1081–1091.

Kellermanns, F. W., Eddleston, K. A., Barnett, T., & Pearson, A. W. (2008). An exploratory study of family member characteristics and involvement: Effects on entrepreneurial behaviour in the family firm. *Family Business Review*, *21*(1), 1–14.

Kennedy, P. (1982). *The rise and fall of the great powers: Economic change and military conflict from 1500 to 2000*. Random House.

Kim, W. C., & Mauborgne, R. (2005). *Blue ocean strategy: How to create uncontested market space and make the competition irrelevant*. Harvard Business Review Press.

Kinchelow, J., & McLaren, P. (2002). Rethinking critical theory and qualitative research. https://doi.org/10.1007/978-94-6091-397-6_23

Kirca, A. H., Jayachandran, S., & Bearden, W. O. (2005). Market orientation: A meta-analytic review and assessment of its antecedents and impact on performance. *Journal of Marketing*, *69*(2), 24–41.

Klein, H. K., & Myers, M. D. (2001). A classification scheme for interpretive research in information systems. In *Qualitative research in IS: Issues and trends* (pp. 218–239).

Kline, R. B. (2015). *Principles and practice of structural equation modeling* (4th ed.). Guilford Press.

Kogut, B., & Zander, U. (1992). Knowledge of the firm, combinative capabilities, and the replication of technology. *Organization Science*, *3*(3), 383–397.

Kohli, A. K., & Jaworski, B. J. (1990). Market orientation: The construct, research propositions, and managerial implications. *Journal of Marketing*, *54*, 1–18.

Kortmann, S. (2012). *The relationship between organizational structure and organizational ambidexterity: A comparison between manufacturing and service firms*. Springer Gabler.

Kotter, J. P., & Heskett, J. L. (1992). *Corporate culture and performance*. Free Press.

Kwok, J. T. (2018). An overview of artificial intelligence. *Journal of Cybersecurity*, *4*(1), 1–12.

Laplume, J. B., & Dass, P. (2012). The role of firm-specific factors in the relationship between corporate social responsibility and firm performance. *Strategic Management Journal*, *33*(8), 1022–1047.

Lavie, D., Stettner, U., & Tushman, M. L. (2010). Exploration and exploitation within and across organizations. *Academy of Management Annals*, *4*(1), 109–155.

Lawrence, P. R., & Lorsch, J. W. (1967). Differentiation and integration in complex organizations. *Administrative Science Quarterly*, *12*(1), 1–47.

Leavy, B. (2004). Corporate strategy and innovation: A review. *Journal of Business Strategy*, *25*(5), 24–34.

Lei, D., Hitt, M. A., & Bettis, R. A. (1996). Dynamic capabilities and strategic management. *Strategic Management Journal*, *17*(S2), 171–195.

Leiponen, A., & Helfat, C. E. (2010). Innovation objectives, knowledge sources, and the benefits of innovation. *Strategic Management Journal*, *31*(6), 636–658.

Leonard-Barton, D. (1992). Core capabilities and core rigidities: A paradox in managing new product development. *Strategic Management Journal*, *13*(11), 1–125.

Lester, S. (1999). An introduction to phenomenological research. *Stan Lester Developments*. http://www.sld.demon.co.uk/resmethy.pdf

Levinthal, D., & March, J. G. (1993). The myopia of learning. *Strategic Management Journal*, *14*, 95–112.

Li, X., Li, Y., & Wu, J. (2018). How organizational learning influences business performance: Evidence from emerging markets. *Journal of Management Studies*, *55*(1), 1–25.

Li, Y., & Yang, Y. (2018). The impact of organizational culture on OA: Evidence from China. *Asia Pacific Journal of Management*, *35*(1), 33–54.

Lichtenthaler, U., & Ernst, H. (2016). The impact of organizational culture on innovation management. *Journal of Business Research*, *69*(2), 616–624.

Linhart, A., Röglinger, M., & Stelzl, K. (2020). A project portfolio management approach to tackling the exploration/exploitation trade-off. *Business & Information Systems Engineering*, *62*, 103–119.

Liu, Y., Liu, C., & Wang, S. (2018). The impact of organizational culture on innovation: Evidence from China. *Journal of Business Research*, *85*, 244–253.

Lubatkin, M. H., Simsek, Z., Ling, Y., & Veiga, J. F. (2006). Ambidexterity and performance in small- to medium-sized firms: The pivotal role of top management team behavioral integration. *Journal of Management*, *32*, 1–27.

Lubatkin, M. H., Simsek, Z., Ling, Y., & Veiga, J. F. (2016).

Maier, M., Meyer, C., & Saloma, V. (2003). The role of organizational culture in innovation. *International Journal of Innovation Management*, *7*(4), 423–435.

Malhotra, N., & Birks, D. (2006). *Marketing research: An applied approach* (updated 2nd European ed.). Prentice Hall.

Malhotra, N. K. (2019). *Basic marketing research* (4th ed.). Pearson.

Mandhani, S. (2010). Innovation and firm performance: A study of small and medium enterprises in India. *International Journal of Business and Management*, *5*(4), 45–58.

March, J. G. (1991). Exploration and exploitation in organizational learning. *Organization Science*, *2*(1), 71–87.

March, J. G., & Simon, H. A. (1958). *Organizations.* Wiley.

Maritan, C., & Peteraf, M. (2007). Dynamic capabilities and organizational processes. In C. Helfat, S. Finkelstein, W. Mitchell, M. Peteraf, H. Singh, D. Teece, & S. Winter (Eds.), *Dynamic capabilities: Understanding strategic change in organization* (pp. 30–45). Blackwell Publishing.

Maritan, C. A. (2001). Capital investment as investing in organizational capabilities: An empirically grounded process model. *Academy of Management Journal*, *44*, 513–531.

Markides, C., & Charitou, C. (2004). Competing with dual business models: A contingency approach. *Academy of Management Perspectives*, *18*, 22–36.

Markides, C. C. (2013). Business model innovation: What can the ambidexterity literature teach us? *The Academy of Management Perspectives*, *27*(4), 313–323.

Martini, A., Laugen, B. T., Gastaldi, L., & Corso, M. (2013). Continuous innovation: Towards a paradoxical, ambidextrous combination of exploration and exploitation. *International Journal of Technology Management*, *61*(1), 1–22.

Maruatona, T. (2013). Book review: Foundations of qualitative research: Interpretive and critical approaches by W. Jerry Willis. *New Horizons in Adult Education and Human Resource Development*, *25*. https://doi.org/10.1002/nha.20011

Marvasti, A. B. (2004). *Qualitative research in sociology: An introduction.* Sage Publications.

Mathe, L. (2017). *Business transformation through Organizational ambidexterity and organizational agility* [Dissertation, University of Pretoria].

McGrath, R. E. (2013, June). Transient advantage. *Harvard Business Review.*

McGrath, R. G. (2001). Exploratory learning, innovative capacity, and managerial oversight. *Academy of Management Journal*, *44*, 118–131.

McKelvie, A., & Davidsson, P. (2009). From resource base to dynamic capabilities: An investigation of new firms. *British Journal of Management*, *20*, 63–80.

Mejova, Y., Rivera, R., Alvarado, C., & Haddadi, H. (2019). Towards explainable and transparent algorithmic systems: A review of methods and techniques. *ACM Computing Surveys (CSUR)*, *51*(6), 1–40.
Meredith, J. R., & Francis, D. (2002). *Project management: A managerial approach* (2nd ed.). Wiley.
Merriam, S. B. (2009). *Qualitative research: A guide to design and implementation.* Jossey-Bass.
Miller, D. (1988a). Relating Porter's business strategies to environment and structure: Analysis and performance implications. *Academy of Management Journal*, *31*(2), 280–308.
Miller, D. (1988b). *The Icarus paradox: How exceptional companies bring about their own downfall.* Harper & Row.
Miller, D. (1996). A framework for evolving firm capabilities. *Journal of Management Studies*, *33*(3), 374–393.
Mintzberg, H. (1994). *The rise and fall of strategic planning.* Prentice-Hall.
Moreno-Luzon, M., Gil-Marques, M., & Arteaga, F. (2014). Driving Organizational ambidexterity through process management: The key role of cultural change. *Total Quality Management & Business Excellence*, *25*(9–10), 1026–1038.
Mukherji, P., & Albon, D. (2010). Book review: Research methods in early childhood: An introductory guide: By Penny Mukherji and Deborah Albon London: SAGE, 2010. *Journal of Research in International Education*, *9*, 327–330. https://doi.org/10.1177/14752409100090030903
Mutisya, P. M., Obonyo, P., Ogollah, K., & Njihia, J. (2020). Organizational ambidexterity and performance of large manufacturing firms in Kenya. *DBA Africa Management Review*, *10*(5), 23–36.
Myers, M. D. (2009). *Qualitative research in business and management.* Sage Publications.
Narver, J. C., & Slater, S. F. (1990). The effect of a market orientation on business profitability. *Journal of Marketing*, *54*(4), 20–35. https://doi.org/10.2307/1251757
Narver, J. C., Slater, S. F., & MacLachlan, D. L. (2004). Responsive and proactive market orientation and new-product success. *Journal of Product Innovation Management*, *21*(5), 334–347.
Nguyen, T. T. (2014). *Differential absorptive capacities, ambidexterity & new product creativity: A longitudinal investigation of US high technology SMEs from the attention-based perspective* [PhD Thesis, Cardiff University].
Nohria, N., Joyce, W., & Roberson, B. (2003, July). What really works. *Harvard Business Review.*
Nosella, A., Cantarello, S., & Filippini, R. (2012). The intellectual structure of organizational ambidexterity: A bibliographic investigation into the state of the art. *Strategic Organization*, *10*(4), 450–465.
Nutt, P. C. (1986). Tactics for decision-making in organizations. *Administrative Science Quarterly*, *31*(3), 414–439.
Ntalampiras, S., & Karayiannis, A. (2018). *Artificial intelligence in business: Current and future applications.* Springer.
O'Reilly, C. A., & Chatman, J. A. (1996). Culture as a social control mechanism: Costly signaling and coordinating mechanisms. *Administrative Science Quarterly*, *41*(2), 293–320.
O'Reilly, C. A., Harreld, J. B., & Tushman, M. L. (2009). Organizational ambidexterity: IBM and emerging business opportunities. *California Management Review*, *51*, 1–25.

O'Reilly, C. A., & Tushman, M. L. (2004a). The ambidextrous organization. *Harvard Business Review, 82*(4), 74–81.

O'Reilly, C. A., & Tushman, M. L. (2004b). The ambidextrous organization: Managing evolutionary and revolutionary change. *California Management Review, 47*(1), 17–41.

O'Reilly, C. A., & Tushman, M. L. (2008). Ambidexterity as a dynamic capability: Resolving the innovator's dilemma. *Research in Organizational Behavior, 28*, 185–206.

O'Reilly, C. A., & Tushman, M. L. (2011). Organizational ambidexterity in action: How managers explore and exploit. *California Management Review, 53*(4), 5–22.

O'Reilly, C. A., & Tushman, M. L. (2013). Organizational ambidexterity: Past, present, and future. *The Academy of Management Perspectives, 27*(4), 324–338.

O'Reilly, C., & Tushman, M. (2013, December 30). Organizational ambidexterity: Past, present and future. *SSRN Electronic Journal, 27*. https://doi.org/10.2139/ssrn.2285704

O'Reilly III, C. A., & Tushman, M. L. (2014). Organizational ambidexterity: Past, present, and future. *Academy of Management Perspectives, 28*(4), 321–339.

Pandza, K., Horsburgh, S., Gorton, K., & Polajnar, A. (2003). A real options approach to managing resources and capabilities. *International Journal of Operations and Production Management, 23*(9), 1010–1036.

Papachroni, A. (2015). Exploring the dynamics of innovation in established firms: The role of organizational structure and processes. *Journal of Business Research, 68*(10), 2067–2077.

Papachroni, A., Heracleous, L., & Paroutis, S. (2015). Organizational ambidexterity through the lens of paradox theory: Building a novel research agenda. *The Journal of Applied Behavioral Science, 51*(1), 71–93.

Papachroni, A., Heracleous, L., & Paroutis, S. (2016). In pursuit of ambidexterity: Managerial reactions to innovation-efficiency tensions. *Human Relations, 69*(9), 1791–1822.

Patton, M. Q. (2005). *Qualitative research and evaluation methods* (3rd ed.). Sage.

Patton, M. Q. (2015). *Qualitative research & evaluation methods: Integrating theory and practice*. Sage Publications.

Pellegrinelli, S., Murray-Webster, R., & Turner, N. (2015). Facilitating organizational ambidexterity through the complementary use of projects and programs. *International Journal of Project Management, 33*(1), 153–164.

Peng, M. W., Wang, D. Y. L., & Jiang, Y. (2019). An institution-based view of international business strategy: A focus on emerging economies. *Journal of International Business Studies, 39*(5), 920–936. https://doi.org/10.1057/palgrave.jibs.8400377

Peng, M. Y. P., & Lin, K. H. (2019). Impact of ambidexterity and environmental dynamism on dynamic capability development trade-offs. *Sustainability, 11*, 2334.

Perrow, C. (1986). *Complex organizations: A critical essay* (3rd ed., pp. 200–220). McGraw-Hill.

Peteraf, M. A. (1993). The cornerstones of competitive advantage: A resource-based view. *Strategic Management Journal, 14*, 179–191.

Peteraf, M. A. (2009). Dynamic capabilities: What are they? *Strategic Management Journal, 30*(7), 695–708.

Pham, L. (2018). A review of key paradigms: Positivism, interpretivism and critical inquiry. https://doi.org/10.13140/RG.2.2.13995.54569

Pisano, G. P. (2006). *Science business: The promise, the reality, and the future of biotech*. Harvard Business Review Press.

Pisano, G. P. (2019). The hard truth about innovative cultures. *Harvard Business Review, 97*(1), 62–71.

Popadiuk, S., & Bido, D. D. S. (2016). Exploration, exploitation, and organizational coordination mechanisms. *Revista de Administração Contemporânea, 20*(2), 238–260.

Pope, C., Ziebland, S., & Mays, N. (2000). Analysing qualitative data. *British Medical Journal, 320*(7227), 114.

Porter, M. E. (1996). What is strategy? *Harvard Business Review, 74*(6), 61–78.

Porter, M. E. (2008). The five competitive forces that shape strategy. *Harvard Business Review, 86*(1), 25–40.

Pratap, A. (2019). Research designs in marketing research and their types: Exploratory, descriptive and causal

Raisch, S. (2008). Dynamic capabilities and strategic management: An introduction. In J. Birkinshaw & G. Kano (Eds.), *The Oxford handbook of strategy* (pp. 306–320). Oxford University Press.

Raisch, S., & Birkinshaw, J. (2009). Organizational ambidexterity: Antecedents and outcomes. *Academy of Management Journal, 52*(3), 685–709.

Raisch, S., Birkinshaw, J., Probst, G., & Tushman, M. L. (2009). Organizational ambidexterity: Balancing exploitation and exploration for sustained performance. *Organization Science, 20*(4), 685–695. https://doi.org/10.1287/orsc.1090.0428

Raisch, S., Birkinshaw, J., Probst, G., Tushman, M. (2009). Organizational Ambidexterity: Balancing Exploitation and Exploration for Sustained Performance. *Organization Science*, 20, 685-695. https://doi.org/10.1287/orsc.1090.0428

Ramamurthy, K. (2011). Information technology and organizational performance: A review and synthesis. *Journal of Strategic Information Systems, 20*(1), 1–27.

Reeves, M., & Deimler, M. (2011). Adaptability: The new competitive advantage. *Harvard Business Review.*

Reeves, T. C., & Hedberg, J. G. (2003). *Interactive learning systems evaluation.* Educational Technology Publications.

Reilly III, R. R. (2013). *The cultural inertia trap: How organizational culture can undermine market sustainability.* Emerald Group Publishing.

Reimann, C. K., de Oliveira Carvalho, F. M. P., & Duarte, M. P. (2022). Adaptive marketing capabilities, market orientation, and international performance: The moderation effect of competitive intensity. *Journal of Business & Industrial Marketing, 37*, 2533–2543.

Reischl, A., Weber, S., Fischer, S., & Lang-Koetz, C. (2022). Contextual ambidexterity: Tackling the exploitation and exploration dilemma of innovation management in SMEs. *International Journal of Innovation and Technology Management, 19*(2), 2250006.

Robbins, S. P., & Judge, T. A. (2013). *Organizational behavior* (pp. 253–258). Pearson Education Limited.

Robbins, S. P., & Judge, T. A. (2017). *Organizational behavior* (17th ed.). Pearson.

Röder, S., Fink, L., & Hoffmann, J. (2014). The role of experimentation in organizational learning and innovation. *Journal of Business Research, 67*(6), 1206–1215.

Roglinger, M., Popp, K., & Becker, J. (2018a). The role of IT in the digital transformation of organizations: A structured literature review and future research agenda. *European Journal of Information Systems, 27*(5), 501–520.

Roglinger, S., Overby, J., & Boudreau, M.-C. (2018b). Managing digital transformation in organizations. *Information Systems Journal, 28*(1), 135–157.

Rothaermel, F. T. (2015). *Strategic management.* McGraw-Hill Education.

Rudd, J., Greenley, G., Beatson, A., & Lings, I. (2008). Strategic planning and performance: Extending the debate. *Journal of Business Research, 61*, 99–108.

Rumelt, R. P. (1974). *Strategy, structure, and economic performance.* Harvard University Press.

Sabharwal, M. (2007). Foundations of qualitative research: Interpretive and critical approaches. *Social Science Journal*, *44*, 582–584. https://doi.org/10.1016/j.soscij.2007.07.007

Sambamurthy, V., Bharadwaj, A., & Grover, V. (2003). Shaping agility through digital options: Reconceptualizing the role of information technology in contemporary firms. *MIS Quarterly*, *27*(2), 237–263.

Sambamurthy, V., Bharadwaj, A., & Grover, V. (2007). Shaping agility through digital options: Reconceptualizing the role of information technology in contemporary firms. *MIS Quarterly*, *31*(2), 237–263.

Sánchez, J. L., & Vélez, M. L. (2018). Strategy implementation effectiveness: The role of organizational culture. *Journal of Business Research*, *88*, 362–367.

Schein, E. H. (1985). *Organizational culture and leadership: A dynamic view*. Jossey-Bass.

Schein, E. H. (2010). *Organizational culture and leadership* (4th ed.). Jossey-Bass.

Schmiedel, T., & Brocke, J. (2012). Information systems research and innovation: A critical review. *Information Systems Journal*, *22*(2), 165–192.

Sheffi, Y., & Rice, J. B. (2005). *A supply chain management perspective on the role of the firm's supply chain*. MIT Press.

Siggelkow, N., & Levinthal, D. A. (2003). Temporarily divide to conquer: Centralized, decentralized, and reintegrated organizational approaches to exploration and adaptation. *Organization Science*, *14*(6), 650–669.

Sileyew, K. (2019). Research design and methodology.

Simsek, Z., Heavey, C., Veiga, J. F., & Souder, D. (2009). A typology for aligning organizational ambidexterity's conceptualizations, antecedents, and outcomes. *Journal of Management Studies*, *46*(5), 864–894.

Singh, J., Jain, S., & Sharma, R. (2013). Exploring the link between organizational culture and performance. *Journal of Business Research*, *66*(5), 781–788.

Smith, J. (2018). *Implementing organizational adaptation: Bridging the theory-practice gap*. Academic Press.

Smith, W. K., & Lewis, M. W. (2011). Toward a theory of paradox: A dynamic equilibrium model of organizing. *Academy of Management Review*, *36*(2), 381–403.

Smith, W. K., & Tushman, M. L. (2005a). Managing strategic paradoxes: Toward a theory of ambidexterity. *Organization Science*, *16*(5), 522–536.

Smith, W. K., & Tushman, M. L. (2005b). Managing strategic contradictions: A top management model for managing innovation streams. *Organization Science*, *16*, 522–536.

Stelzl, K., Röglinger, M., & Wyrtki, K. (2020). Building an ambidextrous organization: A maturity model for OA. *Business Research*, *13*, 1203–1230. https://doi.org/10.1007/s40685-020-00117

Stettner, U., & Lavie, D. (2014). Ambidexterity under scrutiny: Exploration and exploitation via internal organization, alliances, and acquisitions. *Strategic Management Journal*, *35*(13), 1903–1929.

Su, L., Cui, A. P., Samiee, S., & Zou, S. (2022). Exploration, exploitation, ambidexterity and the performance of international SMEs. *European Journal of Marketing*, *56*, 1372–1397.

Sull, D. (2010). Leading the change: The role of culture in organizational transformation. *Harvard Business Review*, *88*(7), 6–15.

Sull, D. N. (2005). Why good companies go bad. *Financial Times*, p. 3.

Tariq, E., Alshurideh, M., Akour, I., & Al-Hawary, S. (2022). The effect of digital marketing capabilities on organizational ambidexterity of the information technology sector. *International Journal of Data and Network Science*, *6*(2), 401–408.

Tashakkori, A., & Teddlie, C. (2003). *Handbook of mixed methods in social & behavioral research*. Sage.

Teece, D., Peteraf, M., & Leih, S. (2016). Dynamic capabilities and organizational agility: Risk uncertainty and strategy in the innovation economy. *California Management Review, 58*.

Teece, D., & Pisano, G. (1994). The dynamic capabilities of firms: An introduction. *Industrial and Corporate Change, 3*, 537–556. https://doi.org/10.1093/icc/3.3.537-a

Teece, D. J. (1997). Dynamic capabilities and strategic management. *Strategic Management Journal, 18*(7), 509–533.

Teece, D. J. (2006). Reflections on 'profiting from innovation'. *Economics of Innovation and New Technology, 15*(6), 509–521.

Teece, D. J. (2007). Explicating dynamic capabilities: The nature and microfoundations of (sustainable) enterprise performance. *Strategic Management Journal, 28*(13), 1319–1350.

Teece, D. J. (2010). Business models, business strategy and innovation. *Long Range Planning, 43*(2–3), 172–194.

Teece, D. J. (2018). *Dynamic capabilities and strategic management: Organizing for innovation and growth*. Oxford University Press.

Teece, D. J., Pisano, G., & Shuen, A. (1997). Dynamic capabilities and strategic management. *Strategic Management Journal, 18*(7), 509–533.

Turkulainen, V., & Ruuska, I. (2022). Facilitating contextual ambidexterity in a global operations expansion program. *Project Management Journal, 53*(1), 67–83.

Turner, N., Swart, J., & Maylor, H. (2013). Mechanisms for managing ambidexterity: A review and research agenda. *International Journal of Management Reviews, 15*, 317–332.

Tushman, M. L., & O'Reilly, C. A. (1996). Ambidextrous organizations: Managing evolutionary and revolutionary change. *California Management Review, 38*(4), 8–30.

Tushman, M. L., & O'Reilly, C. A. (2007). Research and development, exploration, and exploitation: Implications for organizational learning. *Academy of Management Journal, 50*(3), 663–682.

Tushman, M. L., & O'Reilly III, C. A. (2013a). Organizational ambidexterity: Academic debate and practical challenges. *Harvard Business Review*.

Tushman, M. L., & O'Reilly III, C. A. (2013b). Organizational ambidexterity: The double-edged sword of innovation. In M. Tushman & C. O'Reilly III (Eds.), *Organizational ambidexterity: Balancing exploration and exploitation* (pp. 3–22). Oxford University Press.

Tushman, M. L., & Romanelli, E. (1985a). Organizational evolution: A metamorphosis model of convergence and reorientation. In L. L. Cummings & B. M. Staw (Eds.), *Research in organizational behavior* (pp. 171–222). JAI Press.

Tushman, M. L., & Romanelli, E. (1985b). Organizational evolution: A metamorphosis model of convergence and reorientation. *Research in Organizational Behavior, 7*, 171–222.

Vazquez-Bustelo, D., Eddleston, K. A., & Rojas, M. A. (2007). Organizational culture and innovation: A review. *Academy of Management Perspectives, 21*(1), 64–81.

Venkatraman, N., Lee, C., & Schilling, M. A. (2006). Managing the dynamics of strategic fit: A long-term perspective. *Strategic Management Journal, 27*(8), 707–722.

Volberda, H. W. (1996). Toward the flexible form: How to remain vital in hypercompetitive environments. *Organization Science, 7*(4), 359.

Volberda, H. W. (1998). *Building the flexible firm: How to remain competitive*. Oxford University Press.

Walsham, G. (2006). Doing interpretive research. *European Journal of Information Systems*, *15*, 320–330. https://doi.org/10.1057/palgrave.ejis.3000589

Wang, C. L., & Rafiq, M. (2014). Ambidextrous organizational culture, contextual ambidexterity and new product innovation: A comparative study of UK and Chinese high-tech firms. *British Journal of Management*, *25*(1), 58–76.

Wang, M.-H., & Ahmed, P. K. (2007). Dynamic capabilities: A review and research agenda. *International Journal of Management Reviews*, *9*(1), 31–51.

Wang, X., & Rafiq, M. (2010). Dynamic capabilities and innovation: A study of Chinese firms. *International Journal of Innovation Management*, *14*(1), 61–83.

Weber, Y., & Tarba, S. Y. (2014). Strategic agility: A state of the art introduction to the special section on strategic agility. *California Management Review*, *56*(3), 5–12.

Weerdt, N., Volberda, H., Verwaal, E., & Stienstra, M. (2012). Organizing for flexibility: Addressing dynamic capabilities and organization design.

Weick, K. E. (1979). *The social psychology of organizing*. Addison-Wesley.

Wernerfelt, B. (1984). A resource-based view of the firm. *Strategic Management Journal*, *5*(2), 171–180.

West, J., & Bogers, M. (2017). Leveraging external sources of innovation: A review of research on open innovation. *Journal of Product Innovation Management*, *34*(2), 261–280.

Winter, S. G. (2003). Understanding dynamic capabilities. *Strategic Management Journal*, *24*(10), 991–995.

Whittington, R. (2016). Emergent strategy. *The Palgrave Encyclopedia of Strategic Management*, 1–3.

Wilson, G. A., & Liguori, E. (2022). Market orientation, failure learning orientation, and financial performance. *Journal of Small Business Management*, 1–19.

Winter, S. G. (2000). The satisfying principle in capability learning. *Strategic Management Journal*, *21*(10/11), 981–996.

Wu, H. (2017, January 1). Exploring the origin, definition and measurement of organizational ambidexterity. https://doi.org/10.2991/icmesd-17.2017.1

Wu, J. (2010). The impact of information technology on organizational performance. *Journal of Information Technology*, *25*(4), 285–301.

Yin, R. K. (1994). *Case study research design and methods: Applied social research and methods series* (2nd ed.). Sage Publications Inc.

Yin, R. K. (2014). *Case study research: Design and methods*. Sage Publications.

Zacher, H., & Wilden, R. (2014). The role of organizational culture in innovation: A multi-level analysis. *Journal of Organizational Behavior*, *35*(8), 1133–1156.

Zahra, S. A., & George, G. (2002). Absorptive capacity: A review, reconceptualization, and extension. *Academy of Management Review*, *27*(2), 185–203.

Zaidi, M. F., & Othman, S. N. (2015). Structural ambidexterity vs. contextual ambidexterity: Preliminary evidence from Malaysia.

Zhang, J., & Yanling, D. (2010). The impact of different types of market orientation on product innovation organizational performance: Evidence from Chinese manufacturers. *Management Decision*, *48*, 849–867. https://doi.org/10.1108/00251741011053433

Zhou, L., Peng, M. Y. P., Shao, L., Yen, H. Y., Lin, K. H., & Anser, M. K. (2021). Ambidexterity in social capital, dynamic capability, and SMEs' performance: Quadratic effect of dynamic capability and moderating role of market orientation. *Frontiers in Psychology*, *11*. https://doi.org/10.3389/fpsyg.2020.584969

Zikmund, W., Griffin, M., Babin, B., & Carr, J. (2013). *Business research methods.* Cengage Learning.

Zimmermann, H. J. (2010). Fuzzy set theory. *Wiley Interdisciplinary Reviews: Computational Statistics, 2*(3), 317–332.

Zollo, M., & Winter, S. G. (2002). Deliberate learning and the evolution of dynamic capabilities. *Organization Science, 13*(3), 339–351.

Index

Note: Page numbers in *italic* indicate a figure and page numbers in **bold** indicate a table on the corresponding page.

FSC
www.fsc.org
MIX
Papier | Fördert gute Waldnutzung
FSC® C083411

Kolibri 360 GmbH
Ferdinand-Jühlke-Straße 7
99095 Erfurt, Deutschland
produktsicherheit@kolibri360.de